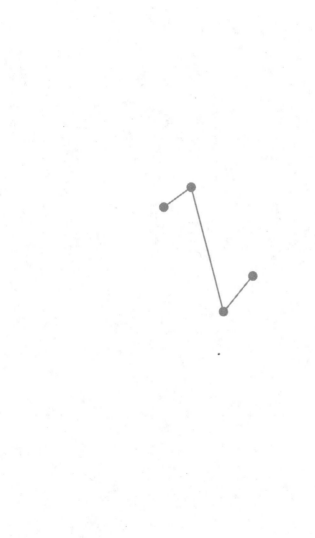

BLUEPRINT
—— *of a* SALES
CHAMPION

how to recruit, refine & retain top sales performers

BARRETT RIDDLEBERGER

Ratzelbürg
PUBLISHING

Ratzelburg Publishing, Greensboro, NC

First Printing, June 2004

Printed in the United States of America

Cover design & book layout:
Bill Foster / Higherwerks Graphic Design / www.higherwerks.com

Library of Congress Control Number: 2004104579

Riddleberger, William B.
    Blueprint of a Sales Champion: How To Recruit, Refine and Retain
    Top Sales Performers / Barrett Riddleberger

ISBN 0-9765867-0-3

I dedicate this book to my Lord and Savior Jesus Christ. Thank you for your eternal grace and unyielding blessings upon me and my family.

To my wife Jodi, I thank you for putting up with me for the past year while I was writing this book. Thank you for your loving support, encouragement and the occasional kick in the pants - much appreciated.

CONTENTS

Foreword

SECTION I

SECTION II

There are a multitude of books on the market about sales, sales training, sales management, and sales growth. The trouble is that after reading them and attempting to implement the strategies, many of the same problems continue to occur in sales organizations. Why is it that new techniques, new methodologies, new leadership tactics, and new opportunities fail to deliver promised results?

The answer is quite clear: *people*. A sales team is fundamentally made up of individuals who all have varying degrees of performance capacity. The various training programs touted on the market have the potential to assist salespeople in becoming better and stronger. There's no doubt that salespeople, like all professionals, need to build their knowledge base continually, and books, audiotapes, and seminars can be a highly effective way of doing that.

Still, there's that pesky little issue of the individual salesperson's ability and willingness to implement those skills. Have you tried sales training, more money. and even threats, yet nothing you do seems to affect the outcome of his or her performance? Are you constantly struggling with the same issues of low sales, eroding margins, high turnover, lackluster prospecting effort, and so on?

Before I address those issues in the following pages, let me tell you what this book is not. This book is *not* another account about interviewing techniques or sales training exercises. It's not about prospecting skills or knock-out closing strategies. It's about human capacity on a level that goes much deeper than selling skills or industry experience. It's about understanding the inner workings of a human being. It's about what it takes to acquire and keep a sales champion; someone who consistently meets or exceeds their sales goals and contributes to the wellness of your organization... meaning they don't drain you or your company of valuable time, energy, and resources. The "blueprint" is laid out for you in a way that explains what you need to know and understand to determine an individual's capacity to perform, whether you're hiring a new salesperson or evaluating an existing one.

I work closely with organizations all over North America, and the problem I hear most often by sales leaders is this: "I've tried everything to build a winning sales team and nothing's worked. What do I do now?" The concepts in this book are based on research. But more than that, this book is based on the experiences I've had in the real world working with numerous sales organizations. Everywhere I go to speak, train, coach, or consult, I keep hearing the same challenges that sales managers and sales leaders have with their sales teams-regardless of the industry. I wrote this book to address those problems.

For example, discovering the answer to the nagging question, "Will this salesperson sell?" lies in knowing what to look for in a salesperson. From research and experience we know that there are identifiable characteristics between top sales performers who sell business-to-business, where prospecting is required.

Before we go any further, let me make one thing clear: We're dealing with human beings. We are the most predictable and yet unpredictable creatures on Earth. There are no absolute guarantees when it comes to hiring anyone-especially salespeople. However, I've had a tremendous amount of success in hiring and developing salespeople because of the observations that I've made and the trial-and-error fixing of these problems for almost a decade. This book is about what has consistently worked in the field with my clients who were looking for a solution, just like you, but hadn't found one. I'll be straight with you: The information you acquire from reading this book may not work for you, but it has sure made a difference for a lot of companies. I truly believe that after reading this you'll know two things. First, this book will confirm what you've known all along-that there's a lot more to acquiring and keeping top salespeople than most realize. But more important, you'll learn what I've learned: that there are specific components that are part and parcel to top sales performers that you can define, recognize, and use in the hiring and development process to increase the productivity of your team. You may have already read every sales book and tried every conceivable tactic to no avail. I promise you that the following pages will open your eyes to concepts most sales leaders don't even know exist.

An old proverb states that the foolish man builds his house on the sand, and eventually the rains come and wash it away. The wise man builds his house on solid ground, and when the rains come, the house remains. You need a strong foundation on which to build your sales organization-one that won't hold up just in the good times but will also work in tandem with your company's goals and objectives through difficult times.

Hiring, training, and keeping top salespeople are no longer a guessing game. The Blueprint of a Sales Champion provides you with the complete architecture necessary for building a winning sales team, one person at a time. I'm talking about a salesperson that is not just energetic, relational, and assertive but also has the internal capacity to back up those personality traits with consistent deliverables.

Being a sales leader is a hard job. Competitive markets, shareholder confidence, and economic instability all contribute to the overwhelming stress of maintaining a successful company. In the end, it all boils down to the quality of people you hire, develop, and retain. When your salespeople do not have a significant capacity to perform, both externally and internally, the problems you're facing today will be the same ones you'll face in the weeks and months ahead.

I invite you now to see the plans for your new organization –the blueprint–that will transform the way you think about salespeople forever.

-Barrett Riddleberger

BLUEPRINT OF A SALES CHAMPION

SECTION I

HIRING SALES CHAMPIONS

CHAPTER 1

WHY DON'T I HAVE SALES CHAMPIONS?

It's the age-old question among sales leadership. Consistently hiring and holding onto top salespeople is one of your toughest business challenges. Many sales leaders lack the necessary resources, education, and training when it comes to understanding what it takes to choose a sales candidate, one who will be motivated to "hunt" for new business day in and day out. The problem isn't a lack of determination or desire to hire the best possible people. The reason most companies don't have a full line-up of top producers stems from the fact that many sales leaders still believe that hiring excellent salespeople is a matter of luck mixed with a bit of hope. In reality, it doesn't have to be that way at all.

So, before we get into what a Sales Champion looks like and how to determine if your next candidate is right for the job, let's look at six reasons why you don't have a team of sales champions now.

1. You don't know what to look for. This statement may seem a little presumptuous, but the fact is that you're leading a sales organization because of your background and experience. You may have been a great salesperson, so the logical decision was to put you in charge of the sales team. My guess is that you probably don't have a degree in human performance. You may have hired hundreds of salespeople through your career, yet many of them never turned out quite the way you hoped. You may have an idea of what you want in a salesperson, but it is solely based on your own experience and the "why" someone works out is often a mystery. If you knew exactly how to replicate your top salespeople, you wouldn't be searching for answers.

But that's the problem. You just can't quite put your finger on the reason why one salesperson performs and another doesn't. The problem is this: You have been looking at an incomplete picture. You didn't know what to look for. That's not your fault. It's been a mystery for a long time-until now. When you don't realize how the "idea" of a good hire is connected to the "inside" of an individual and how deep it actually goes, you typically make decisions on gut reactions. When you do this, you usually base those decisions on a sales candidate's resumé and on their personality-what they say and do during an interview. You may have used a personality test to assist you in making a hiring decision, which is better than simply going off a hunch, but it's still not going to give you a complete picture of the candidate's performance capacity. Personality tests are one-dimensional... people aren't.

Somewhere along the way you may have come up with a list of characteristics to look for, like *assertive, people-oriented*, and *outgoing*, but those traits didn't always produce a top performer. Sometimes they worked; others times they didn't. *The gap between a good interview and a good hire is locked deep inside the individual*. When you don't know what to look for, your hiring decision will always be a toss-up.

2. You don't know what to measure. This reason is very similar to not knowing what to look for. When you have no idea that something can be measured, you will never measure it. Not having a tool to measure human performance beyond the outward appearance gives you only a 50-50 chance of being right. By not measuring things like values and clarity of thinking, which we'll talk about later, the portrait of a sales candidate boils down to guessing. You have no way of making a correlation between the assets a candidate brings to the table and the requirements of the job. The connection between these components significantly impacts whether a salesperson will perform at the highest levels.

Because these measurements typically go unrecognized, salespeople typically get hired for their personalities (from a behavioral standpoint) but are not a good fit for a sales role in your organization. This fundamental lack of knowledge (and tools), of course, leads straight back to the issues you've faced in the past and may be dealing with right now-poor sales performance, lack of motivation, low morale, and high turnover.

Don't feel like you've missed a basic skill when it comes to hiring salespeople. Most sales leaders are not aware that these measurements even exist.

3. You hire when you're desperate. It happens to the most conscientious sales leaders. Unforeseen circumstances leave you with an empty sales position. In an effort to fill the vacant post, you attempt to hire someone as quickly and efficiently as possible to avoid disrupting the sales process. This is not a criticism because you have existing clients to keep happy and more leads to uncover-the process never stops. You have new business to secure, and you have to ensure your remaining sales team doesn't get overwhelmed in the interim.

When you hire salespeople only when a position must be filled, you leave yourself no choice but to hire someone based on a finite number of applicants looking and available for a job at that particular moment. Often that group of job seekers is looking because they are desperate themselves. They are the kind of salespeople who send their resumés to any and every company they can, hoping to secure a paycheck.

The likelihood of finding a sales champion is slim under these circumstances. Making a quick decision to avoid the rumblings of anger and frustration from customers and employees can leave you ill equipped to deal with the outcome. Simply filling the position with someone who seems to fit your needs at that moment may ultimately end up costing you more than waiting for a truly compatible candidate.

4. You hire based on your personal likes and dislikes. Being impartial is easier said than done. It is easy to say to yourself that you will hire a person based on an objective viewpoint. In reality, it is infinitely harder to do. Human beings make judgments about people that can easily be influenced by our circumstances. (You just lost a territory sales rep in the Northeast and you've got to fill that slot immediately. Your current candidate is looking better and better with every passing moment!) Basing a decision to hire salespeople on whether you liked them or didn't like them in an interview can be detrimental to your success.

A salesperson will put on his or her best possible face to impress you. He or she will attempt to convince you that they are just what you're looking for. What happens is that you "fall in love" with a candidate based on an emotional reaction from what you readily see, not necessarily what's "internally" true. That feeling can be misleading, and six months down the road, you may be wishing you could "break up" with your new hire.

These feelings you have about candidates provide you with only a partial view of them. In fact, it can skew the reality of their ability to perform. When the newness wears off and their true capacity is revealed, you may find that they aren't anything like what you thought they were. Just like in personal relationships, choosing salespeople on how well you like them can end up a costly problem.

The flip side of this coin is that you may not be thoroughly impressed by a candidate's interview or credentials and cross him or her off your list. Going off of personal reactions may cause you to miss out on an excellent salesperson for your organization. Any number of things could cause you to discount someone. The candidate may have made a comment that struck you the wrong way, or he or she may not have enough years in sales in your opinion. Whatever the reason, hiring a bad fit or letting a sales champion slip away based purely on personal emotions can leave you with a solid team of mediocre performers.

Sales managers many times overestimate their ability to read people. They don't distinguish between a buying signal and the true nature of a candidate's heart and mind.

5. You either have no hiring process or a flawed process. Either situation is bound to cause you problems. There aren't too many companies who would admit to not having a hiring process, but many truly don't. Not having a clearly defined process means you reinvent the wheel each time you hire a new salesperson. It might come in the form of the questions you ask the candidates. It might be that you have no formalized timeline for offering a job to potential new hire. It might mean that different managers have their own unique ways of making a decision. Whatever it is, a fundamentally undefined hiring process will yield unsatisfactory results. It also offers no benchmarks for successful hiring in the future.

A flawed hiring process can cause just as many aggravations without being as easily recognizable. More companies have a flawed process that just hasn't been evaluated and diagnosed as the problem for continually hiring mediocre performers. A typical scenario that I see quite often of a flawed hiring process occurs when the sales manager has little or no input in the hiring decision. The HR department isn't necessarily doing a bad job of hiring new people, but HR directors and sales managers are wired differently and see the roles of employees through very different lenses. Both the HR and sales manager can be critical to the hiring process. However, this practice can go on unnoticed as a root cause of the problem while the sales leadership wonders why new salespeople aren't doing a better job. I usually recommend that HR and sales management work together to hire salespeople.

Having a process (or lack thereof) that does not meet the needs of the organization can greatly reduce the chances of obtaining high-quality salespeople. Reevaluating the entire hiring mechanism in your company can uncover some answers to the problem.

6. You have unmotivated salespeople. Motivation is a buzzword that consultants like to throw around. Toss a little motivation in the direction of the sales team and get better results. Unfortunately, it's not quite that easy. Motivating and energizing salespeople doesn't simply require *doing* something to them. Motivated people look enthusiastic because they are fulfilling the things they value most. You may be able to entice a salesperson to do things in a different way for a short time (i.e., with some sort of incentive,) but in the end, his or her personal make-up will determine whether or not he or she performs to your expectations in a sales role.

The reasons salespeople may seem unmotivated are as varied as the people themselves. One may not have a sufficient level of energy. Another may have a poor pay plan. Others may be waiting for the sales manager to tell them what to do. Some may even just be embarrassed to say they don't know what to do. They may look unmotivated when in actuality their own personal sources of motivation are not being fulfilled. These driving forces simply aren't visible in interviews.

Ask any sales candidate applying for a position if he or she is motivated, and they will always say yes. The opposite answer would surely end the interview quickly. Lack of motivation in connection to the ability to prospect for new business, stay the course when rejection comes, and follow up and follow through occurs because of internal components that make up every individual.

As a sales leader, naturally you want motivated salespeople– those who will prospect and bring in new business. Knowing what motivates a specific individual gives you a much better chance of doing the things that will spark his or her drive to achieve more. Having that information in advance is key. A perfect alignment between what the salesperson wants and enjoys doing and what the job rewards is the greatest form of motivation.

One or more of these six reasons may be familiar to you. You probably recognize some problem within your sales team, even if you can't articulate it clearly in your mind. In the following chapters, I will detail the blueprint, the fundamental architecture, of a sales champion. This blueprint shows you exactly what a top performer looks like from four distinct angles. It shows you what to look for and how to measure it. It gives you the tools to identify and hire a sales champion at any time. It is an objective process that does not base its finding on anything other than the individual's complete personal make-up. It is also a repeatable process that gives you a procedure to follow each and every time you hire a new salesperson. Finally, it shows what truly internally motivated salespeople look like.

To eliminate the question, "Why don't I have sales champions?" you must first know what a sales champion looks like. You can't tell the square footage of a house by looking only at the size of the nails. You need a blueprint, and this book will show you what it is. Each of the chapters in Section I describes in detail the characteristics necessary for finding and hiring sales champions. In Section II, you will see how to discover and develop any sales champions you may have on your sales staff.

The Blueprint of a Sales Champion is not just another quick-fix, how-to book that leaves you wondering what to do with the information once you've read it. It is based on scientific study, backed up by decades of research and my own real-world experiences. The case studies you'll read about are real people in real situations. You'll be able to identify with many of the scenarios when you consider some of your current and past non-performers and low performers. Whether you're hiring new salespeople or trying to figure out what to do with your existing team, this blueprint will save you money and reduce stress in your life by giving you a concrete picture of what a top producer really looks like–a sales champion.

CHAPTER 2

BEHAVIOR IS NOT ENOUGH

There's a good reason why there are over 1,000 different kinds of behavior style assessments (some people call them personality tests) on the market to choose from. Behavior style is important. It is the outward appearance of an individual. It's the thing you immediately see during an interview. For many, it is a deciding factor for employment, whether you use an assessment tool or your own intuition. You can talk to a candidate for an hour and come away with at least an inkling of what kind of person he or she is. The problem occurs after the interview and after someone is hired. The interview is an artificial environment that lends itself more to the interviewee than it does to the interviewer.

Consider this common scenario. After hours of sifting through resumés, you, the sales manager, select three candidates for further consideration. Each one has sufficient experience, education, and references. You schedule interviews with each person. Your first candidate, Jack, walks into the office in a conservative business suit with a smile on his face. He shakes hands confidently and maintains good eye contact. You have a list of questions to ask, but before beginning, he makes a comment about last night's ball game.

He casually remarks about the score, the way the star player managed to fend off the competition, and how exciting the game was. Both of you were hoping for the same team to win. Immediately, you and Jack are both at ease. You like him already. For an hour you ask questions, and Jack answers. He seems thoroughly composed, and his responses to your questions fall right in line with what you want to hear. You think that maybe this guy could sell anything to anybody, whether they wanted it or not. You conclude the interview with another firm handshake and a smile. You wonder if you should even give Jack the personality test, because you've already determined that he's got a lot of energy and is ready to go to work. You further wonder if you should interview the other two candidates at all. In your mind, the next two candidates have big shoes to fill.

The second interview begins much the same way. A warm smile and friendly handshake wrapped in a sharp business suit. Ellen's first comment is about the photographs on your desk. You engage in small talk and then get down to the business of the interview.

You ask; Ellen answers. She, too, seems supremely confident that she can perform at the level needed in the position. She's assertive, and all her answers are direct and to the point. You can tell she's not going to sit around the office waiting to be told to go out and sell. She says she's very ready to start. Her resumé stands out with many awards and promotions, so it's natural to assume she will repeat those achievements for your company. The interview ends, and you feel pretty good about having two candidates so close in the running.

The third candidate was twenty-five minutes early to the interview. Ron sat in the waiting room, bouncing his legs and checking his watch. When you open the door to ask him in, Ron jumps up with his briefcase with his hand outstretched. He briefly makes small talk, but you can see he is ready to begin the interview. He's really aggressive in his answers to the questions.

Ron says what you want to hear, though. He tells you about his recent accomplishments and his biggest sales. He explains in crisp detail why he should get the job, and you like that. You want someone who will take charge, go after the really tough prospects, fire up the rest of the sales team. You want someone who's going to hit the ground running. When the interview is over, Ron grips your hand again and says, "I'm looking forward to working with you," as if he already had the job.

When all three interviews are over, you pat yourself on the back for picking three great candidates. Now you feel the need to verify what you're thinking. Each one takes a behavior or personality test. The results are about what you would expect based on the interviews. Each one is outgoing and extroverted. Each has the energy to do the job, and they all seem perfect.

You review your notes on all three candidates and decide on the first one, Jack. You wonder a little if you didn't like Jack slightly more because he was first and you are both alumni of the same school, but you finalize your decision because the process has taken so much time and the position needs to be filled.

Fast forward six months. Jack, the one you had such high hopes for, doesn't seem so glorious now. You've put him through the standard company training, shown him all the products, and even sent him out with your top salespeople to help him get his feet wet. At first, he exhibited all the characteristics of a top producer. He learned the products, and his reports were excellent. Everyone liked him and commented on his ability to talk to customers easily.

The problem was that even though everyone liked him, he wasn't selling much. He was very relational and a likable person, but he did not generate leads, let alone new clients. He did not meet his lower introductory sales quotas and certainly didn't after his ramp-up period was over and the real quotas began.

What you thought you hired wasn't what you got. Sound familiar? The interview was great. The assessment validated his personality style, yet you still have a salesperson who isn't performing at the appropriate level. As careful as you may be in your hiring process, just basing your decision on the outward appearance can often lead to disappointing results. You end up with a salesperson that doesn't perform no matter what you do to encourage higher productivity.

Don't feel alone. This scenario happens all the time. What you think you're getting in the way of a top salesperson-someone who will bring in business for the company-turns out to be only partially accurate. There are two reasons for this problem. The first is that most interviews are stacked in favor of the interviewee. A candidate for a vacant position will answer your questions to show him- or herself in the best light. He or she will frame personal accomplishments so you get one impression-that he or she has all the tools necessary to fulfill the requirements of the job. Whatever you ask, the answer will be formulated to convince you to hire him or her.

Many candidates will quickly tell you they sold a million dollars worth of product at their last job. What they won't tell you is that they were working in a $10 million territory and sold only 10% of their sales manager's expectations. A candidate may meet people so well that even you, with your critical interviewer's eye, immediately like them. They won't admit that they can't handle rejection and try to avoid it at all costs. A candidate will tell you everything he or she can do, but they won't mention how poorly they handle stress (even if they knew how to articulate it).

The interview is simply a subjective method for evaluation. As the interviewer, you have nothing to base a decision on but your own personal impression of what you were told. You may be very gifted at reading people and determining whether they would work out, but many times, this method proves to be an inadequate and inconsistent measure of a person's full capabilities (of lack thereof). You could get lucky and hire a sales champion, but it would be just that-luck. When your organization's success depends on how well your sales team sells its products and services, it's a little risky to base hiring decisions on such an incomplete picture.

The second reason for this case of mistaken identity fundamentally revolves around the hard fact that a personality test or behavior profile will only show you the external shell of an individual's personality. There are lots of people who are assertive, people-oriented, and driven who make only marginal salespeople. With the task of hiring salespeople, you probably have some idea about what you're looking for. The stereotype of a salesperson is easily recognized on the outside-friendly, outgoing, personable, assertive, driven, and so on. You see this kind of profile from the behavior assessments. That's what they are designed to do, and there's nothing wrong with measuring a candidate's behavior style. It is an integral part of who will eventually be in that sales position, but it is only one piece of the puzzle.

By using a behavior assessment, there's no question that you have a leg up on those who use nothing. As I mentioned in the last chapter, many hiring decisions have been made based on limited knowledge of what to look for and what to measure. But it takes more than a personality test and an interview to determine if a sales candidate will perform . . . much more.

In addition to behavior style, we will take a hard look at the other measures required for the complete picture of a salesperson, which are cognitive structure, values structure, and selling skills. This combination of measurements gives you an in-depth understanding of an individual's capacity to perform in a sales role. The behavior style tells you how a salesperson sells. Cognitive structure tells you if a salesperson will sell. Value structure tells you why a salesperson sells, and selling skills tell you if a salesperson has the necessary understanding of the complex, consultative sales process.

By these four components you get both an accurate *and* complete assessment of whether or not a sales candidate will be a top producer if you hire him or her. Many assessment devices on the market do not go into this much depth in evaluating a person. It is imperative, though, to understand all four and be able to determine whether a candidate is qualified for your organization on all levels. Otherwise, you'll often end up with a salesperson on your staff that doesn't sell at high levels even though he or she looks right on the outside.

These are the measurements we use to help clients hire, develop, and retain sales champions. This is not an absolute, and we offer no 100% guarantee. But there is no denying the success we've had in reducing turnover and poor sales performance and increasing the odds of our clients achieving their unique sales objectives. Our experience in the real world of professional selling tells us that day in and day out. Let's get started.

Behavior Style
Because behavior style is the easiest component to see, we'll begin here. I'll show you what the four different styles look like, and what you're looking for in a sales champion.

Behavior style is what you see on the outside of every individual. Everyone of us has a certain make up that determines how we will act and react to others. Behavior is like the exterior of a house. By looking at it, you can determine quite a number of things, but you can't tell how many bedrooms that house has or how solid the wiring is. The internal components that are the underpinnings of a solid construction can't be seen by walking around the yard.

Because your first impressions are made based on what you see, we will start with definitions of the four behavior styles: the Doer, the Talker, the Pacer, and the Controller. These styles are very distinct from each other, and all of them have their merits. Every style can sell; however, when you factor in prospecting to the sales role, it narrows down the style that best fits the job requirements

The Doer behavioral style directs others. People who exhibit this style are aggressive and results-oriented. They want to make things happen. They like a challenge, and they probably won't wait on you to be told what to do. They are very direct in their approach to selling. They would be the kind of people you would call go-getters. They have a sense of urgency about all they do. They display assertiveness, and they're always on the move. As outside salespeople, Doers have the assertiveness to prospect for business.

The Talker behavioral style relates to others. People who exhibit this style are typically charming and people-oriented. They can easily carry on a conversation with almost anyone. They are energetic and persuasive, and these characteristics can put others at ease. They win over the people around them and are usually comfortable meeting strangers. They are the kind of people you as a sales manager probably like being around, and they enjoy the attention of multiple connections. They seek status and will tend to conduct themselves in a manner that will elevate their position. As outside salespeople, Talkers typically enjoy the idea of meeting new prospects.

The Pacer behavioral style accommodates others. People who exhibit this style are patient and easy-going. They are loyal in their personal and professional activities. They can be counted on to complete tasks they are given, though they prefer to do one thing at a time. They will perform their duties in a methodical and systematic manner and won't mind waiting on others before proceeding. They also seek security by following a logical progression through to completion. They won't usually rock the boat. As outside salespeople, Pacers give others plenty of time to make a decision.

The Controller behavioral style assesses others. People who exhibit this style are factual and precise. They like to know as much information as possible before moving forward on a decision. They come across as cool and distant to others because they are more reserved than most. They also want order and a sense of continuity in every process they are required to follow. They are quality-conscious and want every "*i*" dotted and every "*t*" crossed. As outside salespeople, Controllers care about the details.

As you can see, not all of the behavior profiles are an ideal fit when it comes to a salesperson's ability to initiate relationships and generate new leads on a consistent basis. When you conduct interviews, you will notice a person's style, at least partially. You have probably seen candidates who fit each of these profiles. They all can work as salespeople, but they typically won't all be sales champions. In Figure 1, you will see a version of the behavior style profile of a sales champion.

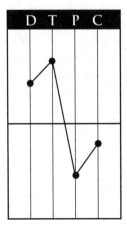

Figure 1. Typical Sales Champion behavior style

A sales champion's behavior profile is often a combination of the Doer and Talker styles. There are several reasons for this. First, to be able to perform in a sales role, an important characteristic one must have is energy if prospecting is a vital component of the role. That may sound obvious, but there are salespeople in almost every company who do not have the necessary level of energy to go out in the field, initiate new relationships, and bring in new business day after day. This kind of energy must be a natural part of who a salesperson is. A sales champion isn't going to need to be told to be energetic. He or she is energetic because they are wired that way.

A sales champion will be comfortable in an environment where there is some amount of risk and change. They see the job of selling as a challenge that gives them a strong sense of accomplishment when a sale is made. Sales champions like achieving goals and enjoy the attention that meeting and exceeding them brings with it.

This is the kind of person you're looking for when you hire new salespeople. The difficulty lies not in knowing that you're searching for a high-energy candidate; the difficulty is that a person's behavior style only tells you how that person will sell. When all you have to base your hiring decisions on is behavior style, you end up getting an incomplete picture. A person may have all the energy in the world as long as he or she is motivated to use it, but a behavior style profile doesn't show you what drives a person to act or how clearly he or she thinks.

Consider our metaphor of the house again. Basing judgments for employment solely from how a person acts (either in an interview or through a behavior-only assessment) is like purchasing a home based on the roof and the siding. The exterior is undoubtedly critical to the decision, but the foundation on which that external component rests is fundamentally what makes it a good choice.

Measuring behavior is something most sales leaders do. You do it either consciously through behavior assessments or unconsciously through intuition and interviews, or both. The behavior style a salesperson has is important because it defines *how* he or she will interact with your clients and prospects. It won't tell you why he or she might sell or (if he or she will sell) once you hire them. Your candidate's behavior style must fit with the position, one that requires prospecting for new business, not just "farming" existing clients for additional sales.

CHAPTER 3

SO, TELL ME A LITTLE ABOUT YOUR COGNITIVE STRUCTURE

"So, tell me a little about your cognitive structure." That's not usually something you'd say when conducting an interview if you're trying to determine whom to hire for an outside sales position. Even if you did say it, most candidates wouldn't know what you wanted or how to respond. Cognitive structure is a person's clarity of thinking. It's the measure of a person's focus on certain priorities, attributes, or concepts that are critical to the role.

Look at it this way. Have you ever known someone who "doesn't get it?" They just don't see life clearly. They don't make connections that lead to productive decisions. You may have had a salesperson or someone else who worked for you like this. You may have had to tell them the same things over and over again, but they didn't connect the dots. Perhaps they had problems at home and brought those problems to work. They were always in crisis. Maybe they came up with a lot of great ideas and talked about what could be done, but never implemented anything and didn't deliver results. Any one of these is a good example of a lack of clear thinking. There are people, salespeople too, who don't see things clearly, especially those things that really matter in a sales role.

Likewise, I'll bet you know someone who is a very clear thinker. They can walk into a situation, size up what's going on, and make a very clear and positive decision. They don't live in a fog. They see things from a totally different perspective than the person you just read about-these people have a clear perspective. They can focus on the relevant and leave the irrelevant alone. Do you have salespeople who focus on inconsequential issues instead of their priorities and goals? Clear thinking is a very significant component of the sales champion.

Here's another way to look at it. Think about an air conditioner. An air conditioning unit has a filter, and air passes through that filter. When that filter is clean and unobstructed, the air flows through it easily and the system works well. When the filter is dirty and clogged, air doesn't pass through it very well and makes the whole system perform poorly. Cognitive structure is like a filter in a person's brain. It relates to how clearly they see things, how clearly they process information, and how they prioritize concepts. Therefore, the cleaner the filter, the greater probability of success. If your sales candidate or existing salesperson has a clean filter, and they clearly see and focus on those attributes that are critical to the role, then there is a much greater chance that they will perform well.

A person's cognitive structure is much more difficult to see and understand than their behavior style. It's on the inside. It typically doesn't show up in the interview. A salesperson with a great personality and a poor cognitive structure (lack of clear thinking) is a major reason that many candidates look perfect for the position in the interview and end up never performing up to your expectations. That's important to know because that's one of the primary reasons why you may get caught in the "what you see is *not* what you get" trap. A person's ability to see him- or herself and the world around him or her clearly will significantly influence how they perform (good or bad) in any given situation.

The fact that a person's cognitive structure determines their ability to function in the real world means that hiring a salesperson with poor clarity of thinking, regardless of whether he or she looks like a top producer or not, will result in a less-than-desirable employee. At some point down the road, you will ask yourself (perhaps you already have) why that salesperson seemed so good during the interview and performed so poorly in the field.

You probably don't know it, but there's a very good chance that your salesperson's cognitive structure is the reason you have so many problems. The issue at stake in a hiring situation is whether the candidate will actually go out into the field and consistently bring in new business. That's what you're hiring for.

When a candidate's cognitive structure is unclear, especially regarding some of the critical success factors described later in this chapter, he or she will inevitably fail to meet your expectations. Knowing how clearly a candidate thinks before you hire him or her can make all the difference in the world. No longer do you have to rely on what you see on the outside. You can see in their minds the things that you'd never be able to determine by only asking interview questions.

The reasons people don't perform from a cognitive standpoint are unlimited. If you consider ten candidates who fit your ideal behavior profile and assess their cognitive structures, each one would look different. Each would exhibit various levels of clarity. Some may be unable to see that one action causes a chain reaction of perhaps lackluster results. For instance, a person who is always late to appointments may simply not realize the connection between tardiness and the fact that clients don't trust them. Another person may be great at meeting people on the front end of the sales process but lack the confidence to ask for the order at the end when it actually comes to finalizing the transaction. When the cognitive structure is not fit properly for a sales position, the results will be a mediocre performer. Think about it. How many high-energy yet incompetent salespeople do you know? Hopefully you don't have too many of them on your sales team.

Everyone is different, but not everyone should be in a sales role. The point is that identifying a candidate's clarity of thinking prior to hiring will give you a much better indication of future performance. As far as a sales position goes, a clouded cognitive structure profile is like a person sitting down behind a group of people who are standing on the curb and watching a parade on the street. The parade goes by and the person sitting down doesn't see a thing. Likewise, that candidate will never be able to avoid the pitfalls and perform at the same level that a sales champion will.

Have You Had One Of These?
See if you can relate to either of these two salespeople. The first one I call The Basket Case. The Basket Case always has

something going wrong. One day it is a difficult customer who just can't be satisfied. The next day it a personal issue that's brought to work. The next day it's something else. On and on and on. You hear him bemoaning some area of his life constantly. He tells you how much stress he's under at work and at home. He blames the stress for his inability to complete the sales. You've told him over and over to relax and take it easy, but the next day or the next week, there's something else causing him anxiety. This gets on your nerves, and your other employees are getting tired of listening to his belly-aching. Nothing he does seems to get The Basket Case to understand how to reduce the stress levels in his life, and you wonder what to do with him.

The Basket Case has a cognitive inability to handle stress. The nervousness and worries that he has, both at work and in private, are the reason he will never succeed in a sales role. He is unable to compartmentalize his life to the point where he can function on a day-to-day basis as a salesperson. The Basket Case will hold on to the excuse that stress doesn't allow him to sell more. Many times he will be completely unaware of his inability to handle stress, but either way, you'll still have a mediocre employee on your team.

Can this be fixed? It depends. Some people have legitimate crises in their lives that can change their priorities and their level of performance. However, The Basket Case is one who does not see clearly how to reduce the tension carried inside. In some cases, through self-awareness and coaching, a difference can be made. But don't be misled into thinking that a one-day seminar will fix all of the problems. Ongoing coaching is just that-ongoing. Each salesperson on your team would have to be reviewed on a case-by-case basis to determine if they have enough capacity to perform. If so, perhaps this inability to handle stress can be resolved. For others, it may be a long-term issue that you can't help fix.

I call the next salesperson the Bunny Rabbit. The Bunny Rabbit has the energy of two people. She's constantly on the go. She makes phone calls, visits prospects, sends them product information. The sales manager can't complain about her persistence, but when he looks at the Bunny Rabbit's monthly numbers, he doesn't see all that effort resulting in sales. The Bunny Rabbit will work all day long as hard and as willingly as she can and deliver little or no results. The reason is she's always going after a prospect that has absolutely no intention of ever buying. The trouble is that she can't see where the problem really starts.

If we take a look at the Bunny Rabbit's cognitive structure, we'll see clarity of thinking in the persistence attribute but a lack of clarity on intuition. In short, she can't smell a deal. She can't make the connection that no amount of persistence and sales skills is going to make a difference with these prospects-they are simply not going to buy. Period. She doesn't see that or make that connection in her brain, so she'll chase after unqualified leads week after week. She isn't intentionally trying to sabotage performance. She probably truly believes that eventually these prospects will crack under her persistence and buy something. Unfortunately, they won't, and she'll continue to pursue leads that will never go anywhere. This is yet another "scratch your head" moment. Do you have salespeople who run down bunny trails that lead nowhere, yet they continue to persist because that's what they think good salespeople do? You can't afford a litter of bunnies. You need clear-thinking sales professional who know when to say "Next!" And you need them to say it as early in the sales process as possible.

Now, you've probably run into one or both of these types of salespeople over the years. Nothing you asked in their interviews and none of their responses gave you any indication that they would perform in this manner. Even if you were to ask a candidate how he or she handles stress, all you have to go on is the response. Obviously they will not tell you they can't deal with stress. The same goes for the second scenario. No one would tell you in an interview that he or she is lacking in the intuition department. A candidate will spend time telling you how diligent he or she is in going after the really tough prospects. It would be hard not to be impressed by that. Yet as I said before, cognitive structure plays a significant role in a salesperson's capacity to perform and determining clarity of thinking is a vital part of the hiring and developmental process.

Again, the reason these salespeople get hired in the first place is that they look like the ideal candidate-they fit the image of the sales superstar you have in your mind. Their behavior profile looks perfect. They have the outward appearance of a sales champion. They have the assertiveness, the drive, and the ambition, but when you take a look at the inside, you see a totally different person. It's like seeing a brand-new house that has insufficient internal wiring. You might think the house was exactly what you're looking for until you walk through the front door. You wouldn't buy a house if the lights, air conditioning, and heater didn't work, so why hire a salesperson without checking out his or her internal wiring?

Will this salesperson do the job? That's the big question on your mind when you're considering a sales candidate. Knowing a candidate's cognitive structure to ensure that what you've seen is actually what you'll get significantly reduces making the wrong decision. A person's cognitive structure is extremely complex, but there are several critical success factors to consider. At my firm, we measure over eighty different cognitive attributes of every sales candidate we help our clients hire. We've found there are a number of key factors to a sales champion's profile that are critical to success. They are self-starting ability, goal directedness, results orientation, personal accountability, handling stress factors, and handling rejection. There are many more (like intuition), but for the purposes of this book, we'll cover these six so you'll get an idea of the direct impact these have on the success of your organization.

As you read the next section, you may recognize the lack of these attributes in some of your sales team. If a salesperson is not cognitively structured in this way, there will be roadblocks to his success at some point. In Section II of the book, I discuss the developmental side of your team and what to do about non-performers.

Self-Starting Ability
Self-Starting Ability is the capacity of a salesperson to direct their energy towards the completion of a goal without an external

mechanism – like you, their sales manager. How many high-energy salespeople have you hired that needed a jolt from a cattle prod everyday to get them going? Sales professionals, especially those that must prospect for new business, must be self-starters if they are to be successful.

Ironically, many sales managers hire high-energy salespeople with the assumption that they possess a self-starting ability–and many don't. Energy level and self starting ability are not the same thing. The former is a behavioral trait, but the latter is a cognitive capacity. You can have one without the other. Your objective is to hire and keep salespeople who possess both if they have to prospect and generate new business.

Goal Directedness

Sales champions know where they are going. They have a strategic mindset that allows them to formulate a plan of action and follow it. They don't let obstacles stand in the way of their activities. By concentrating on the larger picture of how everything fits together, they can navigate effectively through situations that might otherwise hinder their progress. Without the ability to stay focused to the goals, circumstances can bog down the process. When this attribute is not clear, you get salespeople who always need a manager to help them set goals and then keep them focused on those goals. This can take a great deal of your time and energy to fill a gap that shouldn't be there. You should have salespeople who can understand the goals without your constant intervention. This does not mean that salespeople don't need to be coached. It means that you shouldn't have to continually reinforce what they should already know.

Results Orientation

Sales champions have a cognitive ability to bring about closure. They can identify the actions necessary to move them through the process to obtain the desired result. This characteristic is extremely important. It is coupled with goal directedness. Knowing what the goal is and how to arrive there in the most efficient and profitable manner possible gives sales champions an edge over their competitors who struggle to finish what they start. Salespeople who are weak in this area can lose countless sales because they don't focus on all of the components attributed to achieving results.

Personal Accountability

Personal accountability is the measure of one's ability to be responsible for their decision and actions and not placing blame on others for their own poor performance. Do you have salespeople who deliver more excuses than sales? And when they do, do they blame other people or circumstances beyond their control for their failure instead of themselves? You're not alone.

Many sales mangers are plagued by this one simple fact—their salespeople lack personal accountability. Wouldn't you much rather have a salesperson who will say that they weren't prepared for an appointment and that they were the reason that they lost the sale? Now you can work on the problem instead of debating who is at fault. Sales champions are personally accountable and will own up to failures and then proactively work towards preventing the same mistake from happening again.

Handling Stress

Sales champions know how to compartmentalize life. They don't let their personal lives bleed into their professional lives. Likewise, they can leave the office and enjoy other activities like family and friends. Having the ability to handle stress appropriately by properly diffusing inner tension is a critical attribute of success. The ability to handle stress is not situational, like meeting a deadline for an important client. It is an ongoing activity that allows sales champions to stay mentally focused regardless of what occurs in their lives. When salespeople aren't able to do this, stress can build up and performance suffers.

Handling Rejection

Sales champions have the ability to deal with prospects who say no. They can be rejected by a prospect and the next minute pick up the phone again and call someone else. They don't look at the rejection as a personal affront, and they don't internalize it. Handling rejection well allows sales champions to continue pursuing qualified leads through the sales process without getting bogged down in feeling sorry for themselves because someone was blunt, rude, or didn't buy. Salespeople who don't handle rejection well will slowly begin to find anything and everything to do but prospect. The inability to handle rejection will quickly show up in their performance.

Don't assume that a "Type-A" personality candidate can handle rejection either. I've seen too many so-called bulldogs wilt like a flower at the first sign of rejection. I'm sure you have, too. Again, a salesperson's behavior style or personality does not equate to their clarity of thinking. These are two very different aspects of a salesperson's make-up.

Looking that these six attributes, it's easy to see the value of employing salespeople with these qualities. You don't have to be convinced that these are the kind of salespeople you want on your team. The trouble with getting them is that none of these components can be perceived from the interview or resumé. Instead, it is this aspect of an individual's make-up that reveals more about how well they will perform than personality alone. Taking into consideration whether a candidate can think clearly puts a whole different perspective on the hiring process.

You want your sales team to be top performers. You want sales champions. This means finding people who can clearly see the goals and consistently meet them. It means hiring those who are committed to their roles, and it requires people who can diffuse the stress of life and avoid going into an emotional tailspin when someone says no. These sales candidates are your sales champions, and they will be the ones who will reverse the downward spiral of low sales, low margins, and high turnover costs.

In Section II, you will see how measuring the cognitive structure of your existing salespeople can give you valuable information on why they may not be performing. But for now, you need to understand the other poorly understood component of a sales champion–value structure.

CHAPTER 4

WHAT DO VALUES HAVE TO DO WITH SELLING ANYWAY?

In previous chapters, you learned how cognitive structure and behavior style each plays a critical part in determining the make-up of a salesperson and their capacity to perform in a sales role in your organization. In this chapter, I'll show you how values fit into the process.

Each one of us is driven to act by what we value most. We make decisions based on values. When salespeople don't have values that align with the sales role, there is nothing you can do to make them change. Values are developed long before a sales candidate ever applies for a job. Just like cognitive structure, the value structure of an individual will help determine if he or she is a really good fit for a sales position. It shows what drives them to act.

Let's return to the house we're building for a minute. If behavior style represents the exterior walls and roof and cognitive structure is the wiring, value structure is the foundation. Without a strong foundation, no house will withstand the test of time. Likewise, no salesperson will withstand the trials of going out day after day to prospect and develop new business. The value structure represents the footings that allow the rest of the house to function properly. Likewise, salespeople must have the correct value structure to perform as sales champions.

From the hiring standpoint, a candidate's value structure is literally imperceptible. If you were to ask a candidate if he were motivated, he'd most likely tell you he was. What he won't tell you (and probably doesn't fully know himself) is what values motivate him in relation to others. We're motivated to act based on our own unique set of drivers. A mediocre salesperson just may not be driven to perform by the same values as a sales champion. Knowing what internally drives candidates to act will show you (before you hire them) what kind of salespeople they will probably be in the future.

In an interview, a candidate is going to do her best to sell herself to you. Within reason, she could say anything she wanted. She could inflate her importance at her last job. She could spin accomplishments in such a way that you would be ready to give her the opportunity to generate those same accolades for you. Any question she answered during an interview would have the sole purpose of putting her in the best light in your mind.

We measure values to anticipate whether a candidate will have a conflict with the position and to coach him or her to greater levels of performance. Because you wouldn't be able to see a potential values conflict from the interview, this component of the Blueprint of a Sales Champion model gives you a much better chance of hiring someone who not only looks the part behaviorally but also will back up that style with what motivates him or her to act that way. One of the top reasons salespeople don't perform is because of a values conflict with the position. Salespeople with a values conflict will work in a sales role for a short time, but they will never be able to sustain an acceptable level of performance because deep down, their values are not rewarded by the job. They will either perform poorly or leave for another job.

We measure the significance and variations of six different values. The highest two values are usually what drive a person to act most of the time. The six values are theoretical, economic, aesthetic, social, political, and regulatory.

Theoretical Value

The theoretical value measures a person's drive or desire for knowledge. The chief aim with this value is to systematize knowledge for its own sake. Salespeople with strong theoretical values are concerned with presenting themselves as strong knowledge resources for their clients. They want to discover truth in a rational and logical manner. It is important to them to understand identities and differences. For example, college professors typically have a high theoretical value. They are motivated by the opportunity to provide students with new information, and they derive satisfaction from them understanding and accepting their scholarship.

Economic Value

The economic value measures the drive for financial gain and a practicality of thinking. It could be for status, security, or many other reasons, but regardless of why they want it, making money is very important. This type of person is very concerned with how money is made, spent, and distributed. Salespeople with a strong economic value take a practical approach to securing financial gain. They look at how to maximize their return on investment of time, energy, resources, etc. Stock brokers typically have a high economic value, and so do top salespeople. Generating more and more wealth for themselves drives them to search continuously for the next big money maker.

Aesthetic Value

The aesthetic value measures the desire for form and harmony. It doesn't necessarily mean a person is artistically creative; it does mean that he or she seeks out and appreciates the moments in life that are balanced and symmetrical. Salespeople with strong aesthetic values enjoy the beauty of the moment. Architects, artists, and nature lovers often have a high aesthetic value. They seek out designs and structures that promote perfection, and they pursue the necessary tactics to experience them.

Social Value

The social value measures the desire of a person to give of themselves to other people, even to their own detriment. Relationships are highly prized, and an emphasis is placed on kindness and sympathy. Helping others before helping themselves becomes a fundamental exercise. Salespeople with strong social values will seek out those individuals whom they feel most connected to. Mahatma Gandhi and Mother Teresa probably had a high social value. Each was motivated by serving those around them, and they both spent much of their lifetimes acting in ways that might bring about a better existence for others.

Political Value

The political value measures the desire for power. Competition and risk are seen as challenges to overcome. Roadblocks to success are seen not as obstacles but as part of the true enjoyment of life. Salespeople with strong political values want control and influence, and they want others to know how successful they are. CEOs usually have a high political value. They rise to the tops of companies because their foremost desire is to be at the head and lead organizations by exercising their influence.

Regulatory Value

The regulatory value measures the desire for rules. Order and tradition are sought after. This type of person wants a definable system for life. Regulations and principles have deep meaning. Salespeople with strong regulatory values will be most comfortable in settings where authority is established and honored. Marines may have a high regulatory value. They honor their code, and they're driven to act in specific ways that lend respect to the traditions of the military.

As you can see, people place significance on very different values. In the right field and under the right circumstances, each value would be very important to a person's ability to do a job well. The same applies to salespeople.

A sales champion, on the other hand, has the value structure that backs up the outward appearance. In my experience, sales champions almost always place a high level of importance on the economic value and the political value.

Research conducted in 178 U.S. companies found that 72% of the top performers were motivated by financial gain as their number one driver. It might seem obvious that salespeople would

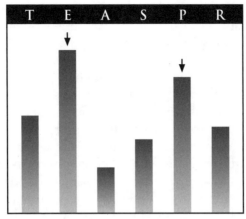

T: Theoretical   S: Social
E: Economic   P: Political
A: Aesthetic   R: Regulatory

be motivated by money, because many of them are paid on commission. But many salespeople around the country are not pri-
marily driven by a need to make money. Have you ever had a
salesperson who never achieved their sales quota, even though
you offered bonuses and raises if they did? Salespeople who are
not driven by making money will rarely perform at exceedingly
higher levels as a result of incentives based on dollars. This does not
mean that they don't want money. It means that they are not
driven to make it because they place greater value on other
things that are more dominant in their life.

The second value that must be strong is the political value.
Again, we're talking about salespeople who must prospect, generate leads, and work in an independent role. Sales champions
want to be in charge of their own destinies and call their own
shots. They want to have freedom and independence to carve
out a niche and take ownership of their positions. They aren't
necessarily loose cannons, running around trying to do things
that run counter to the corporate mission. They are driven to
act by the desire to be influential and important. They seek ways
to obtain status and power. They work best, and even thrive,
where there is a lot of latitude. Micromanagement will run them

off quickly. On the other hand, a salesperson that doesn't have a high political value will typically look to others for what to do. They would rather be given directives than figure out a solution on their own.

Salespeople whose values are stronger in other categories aren't necessarily unable to sell. They can do it, but their probability of consistently meeting your expectations usually goes way down. They won't strive for it. It's simply just not why they get up in the morning. Sales champions have their foundations solidly constructed on these two motivators–economic and political, and that's what drives them to break records and win awards.

Therefore, if your sales position is commission-based, then money must be a motivator for that person to be driven to perform. Money is the reward and they must value that reward for alignment to be achieved between the salesperson and the sales role. If there is no alignment, that is, the salesperson does not value making money where money is the reward, then there will be a mismatch between the two.

From this misalignment I typically see two scenarios play out. First, I see what I call a short-timer. This is a person who stays in the role for a short period of time and leaves because his or her heart is somewhere else. They long to have their values met, and they aren't getting them satisfied on the job. Even if they don't know what their specific values are, they certainly know what they aren't-even if they can't articulate them to you or themselves.

The next scenario I see is what I call the clock-puncher. This is the salesperson that shows up at 8:10 am, takes every coffee and smoke break, takes an extended lunch, mills around the office or hides away in a cubicle, and then is out the door at 4:59 pm every day. Their actions speak volumes about where their heart is, and it's not in their sales role. How many salespeople on your team fit this scenario?

These values are about the key drivers that move people to act. As a sales leader responsible for hiring good salespeople, you want individuals who are motivated to prospect for new business, to be independent, and to be consistent in their efforts to go after clients and leads to make the sale. When a salesperson's value structure does not align with the values of our sales champion model, the probability of effective performance typically declines.

The importance of measuring this component is that values cannot be trained or coached. Because these drivers are ingrained early in people's psychological development, no company manual or off-site seminar will get them to alter their actions. Certainly, they can become more aware and understand what drives them to act. Self-awareness is always a step in the right direction regarding career choices and both personal and professional development. But you can't change them. They're wired that way, and to attempt to change them would be next to impossible.

In a sense, values are the engine by which cognitive structure and behavior are powered. An aircraft carrier won't get very far with a small motor. It can look like an aircraft carrier and sound like an aircraft carrier, but if it can't get out of the harbor, it becomes useless. That's exactly what happens to salespeople who have a values conflict with their role and don't perform. They've got all the pieces of the puzzle in place except the one thing that will determine what their true potential will be.

The other four values—theoretical, aesthetic, social, and regulatory—each can have merits within a company. It's imperative that a candidate's internal driving force matches what the job rewards. Does his or her value structure actually power his or her behavior style? Or will you find out that the go-getter you interviewed had to be constantly prodded to get out and sell because he or she didn't value money or influence?

I remember a client of mine who was looking at a sales candidate and was on the verge of making a decision to hire this person. He was convinced that this candidate was a perfect fit, but wanted me to "check under the hood" to make sure that this would actually be a good hire. I assessed his candidate's values and determined that although he had a high economic drive, his political drive was near the bottom. He didn't value being out in front and calling his own shots. Independence was not a primary driver for him, yet it was critical to the job. As a result, I informed my client

CH. 4 – Blueprint Of A Sales Champion

that this person had a potential values conflict with the role and may not be the right fit. (It was a very independent and commission-heavy sales position.)

However, despite my warning, my client hired him. Within three months, he let him go. My client's first response was, "I should have listened to you." I asked, "What happened?" He told me that the candidate lacked motivation. I've heard this from just about every sales manager I've worked with, so I asked him to be more specific. My client proceeded to tell me that the salesperson lacked a fundamental drive to work independently. He just didn't exhibit a strong drive to prospect. Instead, he waited around for leads from the marketing department and called on existing customers-a lot. Sometimes I hate being right, but my client got the message. Never compromise on quality. Be patient and wait for the champion. Eventually, he or she will show up.

Now, to answer the question at the beginning of the chapter, "What do values have to do with selling?" In a nutshell, values have everything to do with selling because they are the core drivers, the foundation, by which your salesperson or candidate achieves a significant part of his or her personal fulfillment. Let me share a different scenario in which the salesperson had a values conflict that led to his leaving the position.

Another client of mine had a position in which the technician's job was to up-sell services. His behavior style was a Talker/Pacer-warm, friendly, accommodating, engaging, and people-oriented. His customers loved him. They loved him because he went to great lengths to help them. He also had a very high social value, which means he had very high levels of sympathy and was emotionally plugged in to his clients. However, because of his strong sympathy, he couldn't bring himself to charge them for all the work he was doing. He would sell a basic service package and then discover that the client had other needs as well. Instead of up-selling the client, he would simply do the work at no charge because he felt internal conflict about charging them for the additional services. He could have been doubling or tripling the revenue for the company, but he didn't have the heart to do it. Instead, the company's margins evaporated on almost all his jobs.

Fortunately for the company, he quit his full-time position. In fact, he took a lower-paying job so he could invest the rest of his time with his favorite charity. There's certainly nothing wrong with that, but he was clearly not a good fit for the job. That's the revelation that needed to be discovered. He had a values conflict with the sales role. Helping people in need was so important to him that charging for services became undesirable. A drive for making money and exercising power was nonexistent. Part of the position of selling was to offer additional services. Although he could do it, he couldn't bring himself to charge them or to get full price. The need to sell more services couldn't be overcome by his own need to help out. He didn't perform very well as a result.

Looking back, this person had a good initial interview, had good answers to questions, and was technically savvy. As usual, he was hired based on his personality and previous sales experience, yet in the end, the conflict he felt between his internal motivators and the values required for the job led to his inability to sell at the appropriate level. Do you have salespeople like this on your team?

Sadly, this scenario happens frequently because what you see in an interview shows you one thing and the resulting performance shows you another. The bottom line is that unless a candidate has a strong desire to make money and exercise influence, he or she will most likely not be a top producer. He or she won't have the capacity to be a sales champion because the things that drive him or her to act are not in line with what a new business development sales position requires. Knowing this before you hire will save you a great deal of frustration in years to come. If the candidate's value structure doesn't fit with the position, you can move to the next candidate without having spent thousands of dollars attempting to rebuild the salesperson you thought you hired in the first place.

For the time being, we are going to leave these more complex issues of cognitive and value structures to discuss a component you are probably much more familiar with-selling skills.

CHAPTER 5

WHATEVER YOU'RE LOOKING FOR, I CAN DO IT, I PROMISE.

So far we've described behavior styles, cognitive structure, and values structure, of which the last two are almost impossible to identify through an interview or resumé alone. For now, we'll investigate something you're probably more familiar with—selling skills. I've learned over the years that many sales leaders place a great deal of importance on selling skills—the candidate's understanding of the sales process—as a significant part of their hiring decision. Bottom line: If a person doesn't know how to sell, then why in the world would you hire him or her? Makes sense. Isn't it as simple as that? No selling skills, no job! Not quite, but let me explain.

I agree that selling skills are important, but as you've read through this book, they take a back seat to the other capacities we've discussed. There's no question that selling skills are absolutely critical to the sales role. Sales training, if done well, can add great value to your sales team. However, there's more to a top performer than just the skills they possess. Success is truly a function of who a person is, not just what they know.

Therefore, my goal is to put selling skills in proper perspective as it relates to hiring and developing sales professionals. The other three capacities I've discussed are critical, as are selling skills. However, selling skills are the easiest to teach and at the same time have the least impact if you don't have the right salesperson in the first place.

Put another way, I would rather have a rookie with a sales champion profile and teach him or her selling skills than an industry veteran with great selling skills and a behavioral, cognitive, and values conflict with the role. I can teach selling skills, but I can't teach someone to be different than they really are.

Again, most sales leaders live in the behavior style (person-ality) and selling skills world. These two things are what most sales leaders use to hire new salespeople. Behavior style, as I've already mentioned, is the outward appearance. It's what you see on the surface. A face-to-face meeting with a candidate gives you a fairly decent idea of his or her behavior style, even though it may not be backed up by the right value structure and/or cog-nitive structure. A similar thing happens regarding selling skills. Just because a salesperson has experience and an impressive resumé of awards and designations doesn't necessarily mean he or she truly understands the complex sales process or will perform at the same level in your company. How many "top salespeople" have you hired from within your industry who failed to perform in your organization?

In the same regard, a person who has never really had a sales position shouldn't be immediately eliminated from the pool of possible candidates. It all goes back to who that person is as a human being, how he or she is wired and what he or she values. The better job you do of matching up a candidate who's in align-ment with the sales role, the better chance you'll have of hiring a sales champion, rookie or not.

When you interview a potential salesperson, you want to know if he or she knows how to sell. You need to know that the candidate has the knowledge base to understand the complex sales process. You may have run a personality test to validate your initial feelings about whom to conduct further interviews with. So, if nothing else, you intend on only interviewing can-didates who have the behavior characteristics you've grown accustomed to seeing in top salespeople-assertive, relational, energetic, and so on.

Sales leaders typically uncover selling skills knowledge by asking questions related to previous job experience. You might say, "Tell me about your previous experience." The candidate will proceed to do so, but does that really give you any indication that he or she knows the sales process? Not really. A person's answer to a question like that would be completely relative to the situation. You might be enamored by the names of those clients, or you might be impressed with the volume of the business conducted with that customer. Still, the bottom line is that you don't have a true measurement of how well the person understands how to sell. In reality, there are an infinite number of reasons why that candidate had those clients in the first place. Unless you dig a little deeper, you assume that for the candidate to do that kind of business, he or she must know something about the sales process.

That is probably true. Most people, if given a choice on the best action to take in a selling situation, would have some idea. Much of the skills necessary to sell are common sense. For instance, I've assessed rookies who never held a sales position before, yet they knew instinctively that after all the information about the product or service has been given to the prospect, there was a natural progression to closing the sale. But the problem occurs when the salesperson doesn't know what to do to make that sale final.

Basing your decision to hire salespeople on what they tell you about themselves can be very disappointing. The typical situation happens like this. A salesperson leaves your company, and you have to fill the vacant position. You have an intense desire to buy, and every candidate you interview has an intense desire to be bought. As I said earlier, the interview is stacked in the favor of the candidate. When you ask questions about previous work experience to determine how well they know how to sell, most of the time their answers will be designed to fit in line with what you want to hear. Remember, you've got to get that position filled as soon as possible, and the candidate knows he or she only has one chance to prove he or she is the best person for the job. When a candidate tells you he was a million-dollar producer at his last job, it sounds impressive. There's nothing inherently negative about being a million-dollar producer, but how that person arrived at that number is more the key that unlocks a candidate's knowledge of the sales process. What are the circumstances surrounding that seemingly large volume?

It may seem as though simply asking more targeted questions

would give you a more accurate assessment of a candidate's skill level. In one sense, that's true. The more probing questions you can ask about someone's knowledge of selling, the better, but it's not just a matter of answers to questions. It's still based on subjectivity on the part of both the interviewer and the interviewee. The candidate isn't usually trying to be misleading in his or her responses, but the combination of two individual humans interacting in a situation that has the potential to alleviate two problems (the company's need for a salesperson and a salesperson's need for a job) makes it very difficult to remain objective.

I actually use a sales test, which is part of the assessment described in the last chapter, to determine a salesperson's level of selling skills because I want to reduce the amount of subjectivity in the decision. It isn't based on subjective questions that can be answered in such a way that sounds like the perfect answer. A salesperson answers 54 questions related to the complex sales process. He or she selects what they feel to be the most effective strategy. The score is determined by taking the number of times they chose the most effective strategy and the number of times they chose the second most effective strategy (because under certain circumstances the second most effective strategy is the better choice). I've found that a score of 40 or more shows that the candidate has a good understanding of the entire process. By itself, it only shows how much knowledge a person has of the sales process. Whether he or she will implement that knowledge on the job is where the other components we've discussed come into play. In Section II, I'll show how this measurement can be used to target specific areas of selling skills training. From a hiring standpoint, this score tells you exactly (without any misleading stories of big numbers) how much the candidate understands what to do in each step of the sales process-from prospecting to the close.

Most sales leaders looking for a new salesperson want to know about these first and last steps. You want to know the amount and quality of the leads in their pipeline, and you want to know how much business they are likely to close. Sadly, getting from the first to the last step can trip up many salespeople for a variety of reasons.

It may be a lack of knowledge. Many salespeople just do not know what to do given a certain circumstance. In fact, I remember when I went on my first sales call. I made the appointment and went to see this person. We engaged in small talk from the lobby to her office. I sat down across the desk from her with my trusty briefcase at my side full of demos and brochures. And then all of a sudden, I froze. I just sat there in silence with this woman staring back at me. At that moment, I had no idea what to do next. We just sat there staring at each other for a moment. I fumbled around in my briefcase with some papers until she started asking me questions. I think she felt so bad for me that she literally saved me from complete embarrassment. I didn't get the sale, but I learned a valuable lesson. Very soon after that, I enrolled in a sales training class, and it transformed my career. Bottom line: Sales training will help, if you have the right people.

The good thing about my problem was that I could learn selling skills. It is fairly easy to explain to a salesperson how to ask open-ended questions when he or she doesn't seem to be uncovering enough information when talking with a prospect. Strategies are merely the tools by which you do something. The real issue is whether or not the person will use the skills and strategies once he or she knows what they are. A sales candidate with all the selling knowledge in the world doesn't automatically mean he or she will use that information in a sales call.

That may seem a little ridiculous at first. If they know what to do, why would they not do it? Have you ever asked yourself that question? Have you ever hired a person who had the "go get 'em" personality and loads of sales experience who didn't per-form? The reasons he or she failed to produce a similar sales volume like they did in previous jobs have infinitely more to do with the values structure (what motivates the salesperson to act) and cog-nitive structure (clarity of thinking) than selling skills.

Let's take a look at a case study where the sales candidate's job experience and interview made him seem like the perfect person for the position and one case where a candidate was elim-inated due to lack of previous job experience. Both scenarios show how the level of selling skills can be misleading.

Bill And The Case Of "But I Was Great At My Last Job"

Robert has an impressive resumé. He has worked in Bill's industry for ten years and has only been downsized due to a recent company merger. Upon reviewing his application, Bill decides to interview Robert. He comes to the interview with enthusiasm and drive. He has that "killer instinct" look about him. Bill is immediately impressed with his easy manner in communicating. In fact, after ten minutes, he finds himself really liking Robert. He's personable guy, and Bill is eager to discuss his work history.

He notices on Robert's resumé that last year he was awarded the Salesperson of the Year award and decides to begin there with his questions. Through the course of his answer, he tells Bill he was the number one salesperson the last two years in a row and was in the top three in the company for the past six years. It's difficult not to be enamored by the numbers. A million-dollar producer is just what Bill needs, plus Robert has industry experience. He thinks he's found the ideal candidate because Robert only left the last company because of circumstances over which he had no control. The likelihood of him jumping in and getting down to business is almost guaranteed.

The interview proceeds, and the longer Bill talks to Robert the more he likes him and the more he seems ready to start working. Bill gives him a behavior profile, which shows he's got the classic type A behavior style. After conducting several more interviews with other candidates, Bill decides that Robert is head and shoulders above the competition in both experience and personality. Bill hires him, much to his satisfaction at filling the position so smoothly.

Robert goes through the standard company product training and makes a few rounds with other salespeople on the team. He told Bill during his interview that he felt confident that many of his previous clients would come with him when he switched companies, so Bill lets him loose to draw those clients away from the competition, as well as drum up new business.

All goes well for a month or two, and then Bill notices Robert isn't delivering those existing clients as fast as he thought he should. Bill expected an immediate strong showing once the initial product training was over. He knew Robert was familiar with the products, and being the number one salesperson just one year ago, he just assumed that Robert would fly to the top of the sales team, especially with all that existing client base he claimed to bring with him.

If I had the opportunity to work with Bill during the hiring process, I would have evaluated Robert's cognitive and value structure and discovered some interesting facts. Robert's motivators are not money or power; he isn't goal-directed or a self-starter; and he can't handle rejection. In fact, as far as prospecting goes, Bill hasn't seen him making nearly the calls of some of the other salespeople. After a heart-to-heart talk, all that business Robert told Bill he had generated at his last job had a lot more to do with the fact that his sales manager gave him a territory that had been previously developed by another salesperson who retired the same year Robert was hired. It was true that Robert managed the five largest accounts for the company, but he had absolutely nothing to do with getting that business on his own. Robert was an order taker, and because he was so good at talking to people, his annual rounds to renew clients always went well.

Robert wasn't attempting to deceive Bill in the interview at all. He was simply telling Bill exactly what he wanted to hear *and* what Robert himself believed. When he wasn't able to convert those existing clients to a new company or prospect for completely new business, it wasn't an issue of lying that caused the problem. It was more a function of the subjective nature of the interview. When Bill asked what he did at his last job, Robert told him, and it was true–he had the five largest accounts. Outside the context of the situation though, it didn't really mean anything in terms of future performance. And now Bill's stuck with a salesperson he spends too much time scratching his head over, wondering where he went wrong...and spending too much money with no return on investment.

Let's take a look at another case where the opposite happens.

Sally and the Case of Mistaken Identity

Sally is a recent college graduate. She received her degree in business administration and was top in her class from a prestigious university. Though she has never had a sales position before, Paul decides to interview her to see if she might be good for the position. Paul's always told himself he wouldn't mind having some youthful energy to spark other members of his team.

Sally has boundless energy. She is so ready to come to work at her first real job that she makes a very good impression on Paul. The problem is that he has to balance the personality with some level of experience. He asks questions, hoping to discover some hidden quality that will tell him whether she would be easy to teach. For the most part, she does a good job, and Paul is impressed that a college grad could be so composed at such a young age. He even goes so far as to give her the behavior profile, and it comes back strong. She's assertive and people-oriented. She's friendly, yet driven.

Still, in the back of his mind, Paul's concerned that Sally's never been in a similar position before. The closest she's come to a sales position was working part-time through college in an upscale women's clothing store. Through the course of the interview, Paul can tell that Sally is doing her best to maximize the short job history she has. In a way he feels for her, but unfortunately, he's concerned about taking a risk with such an inexperienced person.

In the end, Paul chooses someone else for the position who has some background in selling. He sends Sally a personal note telling her good luck with the job search. It makes him feel better. What he doesn't know and will never know is that he just rejected a sales champion.

Again, if I had the chance to evaluate Sally, Paul would have discovered that his candidate had the right behavior style necessary to go out and sell every day, which Paul gathered from the behavior-only profile. However, she also has the sales champion values and cognitive structures to back them up. She's motivated by making money and being independent. She's also results-oriented, committed to selling, and deals with stress extremely well. The only thing Sally is missing is some experience. In fact, her actual knowledge of the complex sales process is above average. She's able to understand the concepts necessary to sell, even though she's never held a sales position or had any formal sales training.

In some cases where the position needs a strong industry veteran who can deal with CEOs of multi-billion-dollar corporations, a person who didn't have the skill sets already in her arsenal would not do well. But Sally will become some company's star salesperson once someone gives her the chance to start her career. When you have an opening for a sales position that requires prospecting every day for new business, snatching up Sally will be in your best long-term interests. Sally has the willingness and drive to learn the skills she needs to sell for your organization.

Each of these case studies shows that evaluating selling skills alone based on someone's interview can lead to a decision with a less-than-rosy outcome. The level of selling skills indicates what a candidate knows and understands about the complex sales process on his or her own. That is the critical factor here. A sales champion knows what actions are necessary to complete the process, regardless of situational issues like specific product knowledge or prior job experience. Remember that Robert had all the great numbers and anecdotes from his previous employer, and Sally had no experience, and in the end the decision made with each of them was probably wrong.

Making decisions based solely on selling skills and/or behavior style will always provide you with an incomplete picture. When someone looks or sounds like the best candidate, it will often not be any indicator of how well they will actually perform in a job situation. You must measure more.

You might think that it is unnecessary to evaluate selling skills in the first place if so much misdirection occurs from it. This component of a salesperson's make-up is like all the rest in that it doesn't do anything in a vacuum. Taking the candidate's understanding of the sales process into consideration along with the rest of his or her attributes like values and clarity of thinking allows you to determine whether or not this one portion helps or hinders a candidate's ability to perform. It is always better to have a highly motivated, clear thinker with low selling skills knowledge than it is to have a veteran salesperson who knows what to do but won't perform because of a values conflict or lack of focus. As I said before, selling skills can be taught and gradually mastered by any individual who has the energy, motivation, and clarity of thought to learn. When it comes to a salesperson's values and cognitive structures, the most you can do as a sales leader is make him or her aware of these personal developmental issues. You won't fundamentally change that person's values or clarity of thinking, but awareness is a step in the right direction.

So, what do sales champions need in terms of selling skills? Sales champions understand and comprehend the skills required to move through the complex sales process. They have either learned these skills over the years by experience or training or instinctively know what to do. The issue here is that sales champions know where to begin and what to do in each step. If they don't, they take the initiative to find out. Sales champions always work on their game, attempting to build on their strengths. There are critical components to each of the steps of the sales process, and sales champions know how to use them to drive it to a close.

CHAPTER 6

WARNING: CAREFULLY STEP AWAY FROM THE SALES CANDIDATE

A person who applies for a sales position has one outcome in mind. He or she wants to get the job. The goal of securing a position means that everything they do during their interviews will be geared toward achieving that goal. The challenge for you is to understand what they can't articulate and what you can't see.

So much of what determines someone's ability to perform in a sales role has more to do with the internal components of cognitive and values structures than it does with behavior style.

When it is your job to hire new salespeople, you obviously want the best candidate. You want a certain kind of person who will be motivated to prospect for new business with energy and enthusiasm and who can do it without hand-holding and prodding from the sales manager.

That's what every sales leader wants. So why do you not get that kind of performer every time you hire someone new? It boils down to the issues I've discussed. A salesperson with a poor cognitive structure that doesn't allow a person to see him - or herself and the world clearly will never act in the way you think he or she should. Likewise, a candidate who is not motivated to act based on a need to make money and be in charge of his or her own destiny will probably falter when it comes to being a strong prospecting salesperson.

The next two scenarios are examples of sales candidates who looked like the ideal candidate but did not perform at the level of a sales champion because of their unique make-ups. Neither one is a bad person, and neither is subject to living an unsuccessful life. They just don't have the right profile for a job that requires them to sell for a living.

The point of detailing these two people is to show you, once again, how deceiving the outward behavior style can be to future performance. Without assessing the internal components of an individual's capacity to perform in a sales role, you run the risk that the person you thought you hired will end up being a poor fit in the job . . . a costly error. As you continue reading, think if you've hired people like this.

The Expert Who Couldn't Sell
A Values Conflict with the Role

David had everything Ron ever dreamed of in a sales candidate. He was easy to talk to. He was direct and assertive in his responses to questions. As far as Ron was concerned, there wasn't a thing about David that he didn't like. His experience rivaled Ron's current top salesperson, and his past accomplishments were highly impressive. Ron couldn't think of a reason why he shouldn't give David the job because if ever there was a complete package, Ron thought he had found it.

Unfortunately, Ron relied only on his personal intuition because he felt there was no way this kind of person could fool him. Nothing he said gave Ron any indication that he would not do exactly what was required of him, so he hired David based on his interview and references check.

David hit the ground running the very first week. He learned the product so well that he was telling the veteran sales-people things they've never heard. Ron was amazed at how well he knew the information. He heard David on the phone talking to prospects, and he had every feature and aspect so thoroughly memorized and polished that Ron wondered if he didn't develop the product himself. After David had been on the job for eight weeks, he brought Ron a twenty-page report on most of their direct competitors' products and where the weaknesses were.

Being so excited about his aggressive progress, Ron over-looked the fact that David's monthly numbers weren't exactly growing at the same rate as his product knowledge. Ron chalked it up to being new and getting the hang of the job. He figured everybody went through a transition period. Ron discounted the poor performance because David was obviously learning all about the product. He still couldn't believe how much David had absorbed about the product in such a short time.

Then, several months later, Ron decided that all David's product knowledge wasn't getting him any closer to his sales goals. He had made some sales, of course, and he wasn't the lowest producer on Ron's team, but he began to worry that David wasn't selling more.

Ron scheduled some time to go on a sales call with David to see if he could figure out why all that product knowledge wasn't getting prospects to buy. David was thrilled about being able to show his boss his skills. Before they left, Ron got the full report on everything about the prospect that David had been working on. Ron still couldn't see where the problem was. The sales call went well, though David did most of the talking. He answered the prospect's questions as if he had the responses memorized. When they left, David told the prospect to call if he had any questions.

In an effort to give David some incentive for turning more of his leads into clients, Ron tried offering an extra bonus for any closed deals. David didn't seem as appreciative as Ron had hoped, but he was getting desperate to do something to help his salesperson generate more revenue. Several weeks went by, and Ron asked about the sales call they went on together. David admitted that the prospect had gone with another company. A number of other leads were going with the competition, and Ron saw that the incentive (that had worked so well with other salespeople in the past) was a complete waste of time.

In a last-ditch effort, Ron sent David to a sales training seminar. David was more excited about being able to attend the seminar than he had been about anything since his first couple of weeks of training. Ron thought maybe it would spark something in David and get him selling more. When the seminar was over, David returned with a folder full of notes and renewed energy. He told Ron he had really learned a lot.

That enthusiasm didn't last long, and after nine long months of attempting to give David the necessary opportunity to succeed,

Ron gave up and terminated him. The cost of hiring, training, and holding on to David ended up costing the company over $90,000. Ron could never figure out how someone like David could look perfect on the outside and do so poorly after he was hired.

Have you experienced something similar to this scenario? Have you been happy to find a person you thought would be perfect for the position only to discover that he or she ultimately didn't perform the way you thought? The frustration of this cycle of hoping and guessing future performance based on interviews can get tiresome, but that aggravation could have been avoided. Let's take a look at that same scenario, but with an additional component added to the hiring process.

David's resumé comes to the top of the list. Ron wants the process to be over with quickly, and he wants a salesperson who will bring in new business right away. Ron interviewed David, as before, but before making a final decision, Ron asked that I evaluate David's behavior style, cognitive structure, value structure, and selling skills against the Blueprint of a Sales Champion model.

When we looked at his results, David has the classic sales champion behavior profile. His natural behavior style showed that he was energetic, relational, and assertive. Ron validated that from the interview. David's cognitive structure profile checked out as well. He is a clear thinker. He sees himself and the world very well. So far, David looked like a sales champion. Even the selling skills profile showed very good comprehension for the sales process. He actually seems to know exactly what to do in practically any situation.

Now, let's take a look at his values structure (see graph on p.53). David's strongest driver is Theoretical. His Economic value is below average, and his Political value is average. David isn't motivated by money, which is why the bonus incentive didn't produce more results. David is most concerned and will act on situations where he can exercise his knowledge. He prefers knowing information over making money from that knowledge.

Having a low Economic, average Political, and high Theoretical value structure puts David in a conflict with the outside sales position. He is a perfect example of what I like to call the expert. The expert is motivated to act when he or she has the opportunity to learn new things or pass knowledge on to others. Having the high Theoretical value as the primary driver doesn't mean an expert can't sell products. But because an expert isn't driven to make money first and foremost, he or she is not motivated by the rewards of the job–in this case, money. Instead, they find value in the gathering and distribution of the information–not so much the financial rewards that come with finalizing a transaction by using that knowledge. Had David been both high Theoretical and high Economic, then he would be driven to use his knowledge in order to make money. In this case, the salesperson wasn't–and it severely affected his ability to perform in this particular sales role.

The Expert

T: Theoretical   **S**: Social
E: Economic   **P**: Political
A: Aesthetic   **R**: Regulatory

In a sales situation, the expert will be much more likely to spend all his or her time gathering information and imparting information than actually selling. Because the expert has selling skills, knows what to do, and is a clear thinker, he or she is able to follow a definitive pattern, but the conflict with values is what may cause him or her to not succeed as a sales champion.

This values conflict would probably never come up in the interview. An interviewer would be much more impressed by David's ability to explain himself and offer additional information, just as Ron was. Realizing that David may be apt to value knowledge for its own sake rather than as a means to an end, meaning the money he'll make as a result of having that knowledge, gives you a good indication of how he will perform on the job.

In summary, the first scenario is what would happen to a candidate with this particular values structure if he or she were hired for an outside sales role. The benefit, of course, of assessing your candidates against the Blueprint of a Sales Champion model is that you can save yourself the misfortune of hiring this type of person in the first place. Knowing that at some point David will have a conflict with the position can prevent that unnecessary expenditure of $90,000 and the hassle of starting over.

Now that you've seen the pitfall of a values conflict, let's take a look at a similar situation where the issue at hand for poor performance is a cognitive structure deficiency.

Sarah Gets Rejected: A Cognitive Issue

This situation is similar to David's. Rodney had a vacant sales position that he needed to fill. He went through the standard procedure of placing an ad, reading resumés, and pulling out what he felt were the top candidates. Sarah had been in a sales position for the last eight years. When Rodney conducted a phone interview with her, he felt strongly that he'd found at least one person he wanted to interview. At the end of the conversation, he felt confident that Sarah would prove to be as engaging in person as she was on the phone.

Rodney wasn't disappointed. When he met her, Sarah was completely relaxed and professional. The answers she gave to his questions about her past selling experience were succinct and informative. She had received the highest awards from her previous employers, some of which were very strong companies. She had a personable manner that set Rodney at ease. She was clearly ready to start. She told him that she loved a challenge and had in the past always managed to overcome obstacles in her way.

Rodney conducted the remainder of his interviews, and Sarah was his top choice. No one else had the kind of drive and enthusiasm she exhibited, and her references gave her glowing reports. Rodney decided to hire Sarah for the position.

The first day she came to the office close to an hour early. When Rodney arrived and found out when she got there, he felt good about his decision. He thought she was a go-getter. She didn't disappoint him, either. Rodney sent her through all the company training and let her ride around with some of his best salespeople.

He knew she could gain valuable information about what she'd be doing by watching others. The rest of the team really liked her. She was funny, but she knew when to get down to business. She learned all the things Rodney needed her to learn, and when he thought she was ready, he sent her off on her own.

For three months, she validated his decision to hire her. She was getting new clients, and she was going out every day to make sales calls. She was meeting her quotas, and Rodney couldn't have been happier. Other salespeople started joking that Sarah was soon going to be the salesperson of the month. Some of them seemed even more motivated to beat her at reaching this reward, and Rodney watched as a little internal competition sparked the whole team.

Then, out of the blue, it seemed like Sarah's numbers started dropping. She had only been there for a few months, but Rodney was concerned at this sudden change in character. He wasn't sure what to think because it wasn't like she was goofing off. He saw her every morning at her desk, furiously putting together information packets and scouring her Rolodex for phone numbers. She looked busier than before, yet at the end of the month, the results weren't what he expected.

In an effort to give her the benefit of the doubt, Rodney assumed that everyone can't have a banner month every time, so he cut her some slack. Every so often he would stick his head in her office to ask how things are going, and she never gave any indication that anything was wrong. Rodney left her alone, because she always seemed busy.

Several weeks later Rodney found Sarah still in the office at 11:00 am. It had been her practice to be out making sales calls well before 9:30. He thought it was a little odd and asked her what she was working on.

She told him about some upcoming prospects she met at a recent trade show, yet she seemed a little down. Rodney probed a little more, and she revealed that one of her biggest prospects recently told her that although her presentation was good, he had decided to buy from someone else.

He told her that she wasn't going to land every single prospect, but the remark seemed to fall on deaf ears. She thanked him for the encouragement, and he figured it was just a temporary issue. He knew that based on her last few months of work, she'd snap out of it and get back to work.

The days went on, and Sarah no longer came in early. She was getting there on time, but she was leaving later in the morning to make calls, and Rodney didn't see her on the phone nearly as much. He assumed it was circumstantial. He couldn't watch her all the time, and he thought maybe it was just a coincidence that every time he walked by her office door, she wasn't on the phone.

The next month's totals came out, and Rodney was amazed that Sarah had the lowest close rate of anyone on the team. He wondered where his salesperson of the month had gone. He thought about the rejection she got from the big prospect. Was that the reason for the poor performance? It was possible, but Sarah worked so hard through the day that he had difficulty believing she was never going to get going again.

He asked her again if there were any problems, and she said no. She actually increased her activity level, or so it seemed. She left a little earlier for sales calls, and he saw her on the phone a little more often, so he thought it was just a one-time drop.

Sarah did fairly well the next month. At least she wasn't last, but as Rodney inspected the sales she made, he realized that most of them were renewals from existing clients. He wasn't going to begrudge any sales, but he needed new business, and Sarah was supposed to be providing that.

Days turned into weeks, and the volume of new business didn't increase. After repeated attempts to discover the problem Sarah was having with her position, Rodney found out that though she had been active in the office and seemingly full of new opportunities, she wasn't calling on new prospects. She had gone six weeks without generating a single new client, even though she had convinced several existing clients to buy additional products.

Rodney really didn't need any other "farmers." Finally, he decided that she wasn't ever going to manage to get back on track, and regrettably, he let her go.

Once again, what you see is not always what you get. What he thought he hired in an outgoing, driven individual didn't pan out the way he had expected based on her previous job history and the interview he conducted. Has this happened to you?

Let's rewind back to before the decision to hire Sarah was made and consider how she would fare with assessing her behavior, values, cognitive structure, and selling skills against the Blueprint of a Sales Champion model. Her behavior style shows the ideal Doer/Talker profile. She has the energy and drive to go out each day. She's friendly and genuinely liked by most people that meet her. When she meets others, like she did when she meet Rodney for the interview, she instantly has a topic of conversation to bring up.

Her values structure shows she's motivated by money and a desire to be in control. Here again, just like David from the previous example, she looks like a sales champion. She's got the behavior and values that will make her be a good salesperson. Her knowledge of the complex sales process is also above average. She knows how to sell. See her behavior style, values structure, and selling skills in the graphs on the next page.

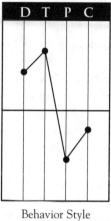

Behavior Style

Selling Skills

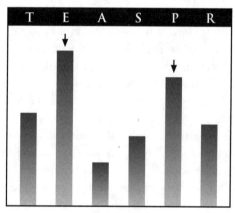

Value Structure

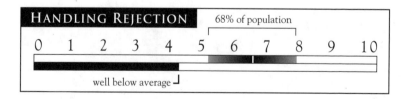

The problem Sarah has that keeps her from being a true sales champion is her cognitive structure. She has a tremendous difficulty handling rejection. As long as everything is going her way and prospects are interested, she will work hard to close the sales. But the moment she gets rejected, she folds. She internalizes the rejection as a personal issue.

As you can see on the preceding page, here cognitive ability to handle rejection is well below the average which is made up of 68% of the population. The ability of a salesperson to handle rejection must be strong if prospecting is a priority in the sales role, because rejection is an everyday occurrence.

Because Sarah cannot see clearly enough to avoid this common pitfall in sales, her feelings about rejection override her ability to act. The internalization of this fear causes call reluctance. Basically, she takes one instance and carries it with her to every other prospect she comes in contact with. Her thoughts are like this. "Since this prospect rejected me, the next one will probably reject me, too."

Having this mentality in an outside sales role can be quite damaging to achieving success. Even though Sarah had the energy and knowledge to sell, the feelings of personal worthlessness prevent her from perceiving rejection in its proper perspective.

The cognitive structure component shows this problem clearly before a person is hired. Obviously, you wouldn't hire a person who admitted to having difficulty with handling rejection, but it isn't something that comes up in interviews. Knowing that a sales candidate has issues with handling rejection can help you decide whether or not to hire them. Without knowing how well a candidate might do this, you end up with a salesperson like Sarah, who at any given time may fall into the trap of spending much of her time justifying why she isn't going out and making calls.

These concealed attributes of a candidate's cognitive structure are just some of the symptoms a poor performer might have that keep him or her from achieving success in a prospecting-oriented sales role.

These two examples of sales candidates who fit the ideal profile of a salesperson (from an interview-only basis) show how important these underlying factors can be to future performance. A sales candidate's behavior style can be completely misleading. In short, what you think you've hired often turns out to be a disappointing choice, especially when you "fall in love" with them during the interview.

Consider this as insight into your competitive advantage. When hiring or assessing existing salespeople, behavior style is only the exterior of a person. When he or she does not have the cognitive structure or the value structure of a sales champion, somewhere along the path of employment, a problem will arise, and you will scratch your head, trying to figure out what went wrong. Heed the advice of the bomb squad who tells you to avoid a seemingly innocent suitcase and carefully step away from the sales candidate.

CHAPTER 7

THE BLUEPRINT OF A SALES CHAMPION

Discovering what motivates people to act and whether they see things clearly makes a tremendous difference in evaluating a candidate's future success in your company. You must get the most complete picture of the external and internal components of an individual to make a good hiring or developmental decision.

Let's recap what we've learned. First, behavior style, the outward appearance of the individual, does not fully describe a person. It shows you how they will most likely act, and you evaluate people based on their behavior style every day, even outside the interview. You do this instinctively because the brain is wired to process and respond to the signals your senses recognize.

When meeting a person, you begin to formulate certain behavior characteristics about him or her. You see that he or she is assertive and direct or reserved and calm. You notice an easy manner of continuing a conversation or controlled, calculated responses.

Until now, with the help of the interview, this aspect of personality has been all you've had to go on to make a decision about whether someone might be a good salesperson in your organization. Even the most seasoned sales leader with excellent perception will only see what a person exhibits on the surface. You've had too many salespeople who looked like the ideal candidate but failed to live up to that assumption to believe that behavior style is only the measuring stick of sales success.

Fortunately, you can now go much deeper than that. When you factor in a salesperson's cognitive structure and their value structure, the combination of the three will tell you more about their capacity to perform than behavior style alone ever will.

When you combine these three components with a candidate's level of selling skills, you get a much more in-depth portrait of their ability to perform in an outside sales role. The components that make up a sales champion are distinct and straightforward. Sales champions are motivated to act by making money and being in control. They have the energy to prospect and initiate relationships. They are also able to see goals and deliver results effectively, and they can handle rejection without internalizing it, as well as compartmentalize their lives to manage stress effectively. Finally, they understand the strategies necessary to successfully initiate, drive, and complete the sales process.

From my experience, sales candidates who aren't closely aligned with this profile may have difficulty meeting expectations. A values conflict may arise that won't be easily recognizable and may be impossible to fix. He or she probably won't perform at maximum capacity because the motivating driver is something the sales role doesn't fulfill. Or, he or she just won't ever clue in to the fact that a poor decision will cause a poor result. This kind of diffused thinking can quickly put a tremendous strain on you, the sales manager, to figure why he or she just doesn't get it.

Behavior style and selling skills are important for sales champions as well. They have to have the energy and drive to go out every day and prospect for new business, and they need to know how to do it. Selling skills can be taught and utilized to increase sales, and, let me stress this fact, the individual has the energy (behavior style), motivation (values structure), and the capacity to see clearly the critical attributes required for success in the role (cognitive structure.)

What many sales leaders do is attempt to train the wrong salespeople. When the behavior style, values structure, and cognitive structure are significantly out of alignment with the Blueprint of a Sales Champion model, no amount of skills training will make someone a better salesperson. Unfortunately, this is the case with a lot of salespeople in the world.

In the hiring process, it is more logical to employ the right people first then provide the necessary training to make them better. This is why analyzing all four of the components we've covered will help provide a much more complete picture of future performance within the sales process for hiring, development, and recruiting.

I can't say that you won't ever hire another poor performer again, but there's no reason you should be living with the terrible odds in attracting a sales superstar that so many organizations live with every day. Having the capacity to acquire a more complete picture of an individual makes your job infinitely easier. Now that you have the Blueprint of a Sales Champion, you can create a benchmark for many of your hiring decisions. You can validate your interviews with clear data about each candidate's internal make-up. Finally, you can begin to assemble your own team of sales champions.

Throw away that bottle of antacids. Sleep well every night. Get up in the morning knowing that your sales team (all of them, every day) truly has the goods to deliver the results you expect. Wouldn't that make you feel a little more enthusiastic about going to work each day?

The power of these measurements can do this for you, but what if you don't need to hire? What if your current sales and/or budget won't allow you to hire more salespeople? That's fine. These same core four measurements are not just a tool for hiring new salespeople. They are also for evaluating and developing existing salespeople. They can show you why specific individuals are performing and why others are not.

In Section II, we will look at how you can dramatically improve the way you manage your sales team, as well as give you hard evidence in helping you decide what to do with them, even if that means making tough decisions.

SECTION II

Evaluating & Developing
Your Existing Sales Team

CHAPTER 8

THE POWER OF THE BLUEPRINT, REVISITED

Most people are a little skeptical when it comes to claims of predicting the future. There's always a hesitation in your mind that it's a little too good to be true. I would agree most of the time. Predicting the future is a risky venture when it comes to suggesting on opening day that the Yankees will win the World Series or that in twenty years you will come into a windfall and move to Cancun and live in luxury.

Those kinds of predictions can be a bit risky to write in stone. The Blueprint of a Sales Champion model isn't like that at all. Through the first section of this book, you discovered a number of measurements beyond behavior style that can help determine a salesperson's future performance within your corporate culture. The four components of the Blueprint of a Sales Champion model aren't magic, nor are they suppositions based on some obscure laboratory experiments.

The power of the Blueprint of a Sales Champion model is completely built around the real-world observations of thousands of salespeople. In addition to being a much more comprehensive assessment of sales candidates, it works equally well for developing your existing sales team.

Through the course of this section, I'll dispel some myths about sales performance in mediocre salespeople. I'll show you how your existing sales team can use the information within the blueprint model to understand themselves more thoroughly and how you as a sales leader or manager can focus your attention and direction in the exact areas in which individual salespeople are weak.

Just as in the hiring situation, knowing a current salesperson's behavior style, cognitive structure, values structure, and selling skills knowledge can give you infinitely more valuable data in developing them to perform more productively.

Let me say this now: The Blueprint of a Sales Champion model is not, I repeat, *not* to be used as the reason to fire someone. It may validate your own observations and ultimate decision to terminate an employee, but it's not designed to be given to a low-performing sales team member as a justification to let him or her go.

There are too many factors that can influence why a sales-person may not be performing. It can be the sales manager's style of management. It can be the pay structure. It can be a dozen different reasons. But sometimes, the only really good choice to make with a salesperson who will never perform is removal from the role, and we'll look at the pros and cons of that situation later in this section.

In terms of using the Blueprint of a Sales Champion model with existing salespeople, it is a way to determine what management practices and development tools are best for that particular person. The fact of the matter is that you may have a sales champion on your team and not know it. His or her assessment may be perfectly aligned with the blueprint model, but for one reason or another, he or she isn't performing at the necessary level. The blueprint model can give you clues to that reason that both the salesperson and you, the sales leader, can use as stepping stones to increased productivity.

Using the blueprint with existing salespeople allows you to discover the unique success factors for your industry. Your industry may be highly technical, and salespeople with a strong drive for knowledge (in addition to money and influence) are the top producers. Your industry may be heavily regulated, and your best salespeople need to have a strong, principles-driven mindset (Regulatory value). By assessing your sales team, you can locate specific attributes that can serve as benchmarks for choosing salespeople in the future. It's really all about stacking the deck in your favor when it comes to maximizing the potential of your entire team.

This section will also show you the value of the sales manager and how he or she fits into the role of the blueprint model. The assessment doesn't work in a vacuum. It provides important information about an individual, but that information has to be acted on by both the salesperson and the sales manager. This interaction between the two with the help of integrated training and evaluation is the only way you will fully maximize the power of the concepts in this book.

What do you do with your sales champions once you have them? You obviously don't want to lose them for some petty reason that could have been avoided. There are some very critical things sales champions need to continue bringing in new business.

Just like the first section, there are many examples of real salespeople in real situations to show you exactly what I'm talking about. If you haven't ever had a salesperson on your team that doesn't fit one of the scenarios, you can count yourself among the lucky few. However, you're probably nodding your head in agreement, thinking to yourself, "Yep, I've had somebody just like that."

The good news is that by using the Blueprint of a Sales Champion model on both your existing sales team and any new salespeople you hire, you'll have the upper hand on your competition. Now, you'll be making a fully educated decision based on measurable data. This doesn't take anything away from gut reactions and intuition. It does provide you with accurate, validated information in areas you can't measure in an interview or in a background check on individual salespeople and how to work with them in a way that gets you the results you expect.

CHAPTER 9

A SQUARE PEG IN A ROUND HOLE

It's a widely held view that some things will never fit together no matter how hard you try to make them. Some things, and some people, just don't fit where you want them to go. Unfortunately, this wisdom isn't often followed in organizations around the world. A mediocre sales performer will never measure up to your expectations, and it's not necessarily that the person is simply average. There are other variables to consider.

Let me first dispel a myth: A marginal salesperson (who does not align closely to the blueprint model) can become a sales champion with enough effort and investment on the part of sales leadership. This just isn't true in the vast majority of cases. A salesperson who does not have an assertive/relational, high-energy behavior style; an aligned values structure (strong money and influence drive); and who is a clear thinker (solid cognitive structure) will most likely not be a top producer if prospecting and new business development is a key component of the job. The fact is that if a salesperson doesn't have the internal and external goods to deliver results day in and day out, he or she will ultimately have difficulty achieving the sales goals.

Assuming that the poor performance is the salespersons fault can be misleading. Just because a salesperson is not meeting sales goals doesn't necessarily mean there's a bad fit. It is important to determine the true root cause of the low performance. There could be a lack of effective sales management. There could be a poorly designed pay plan. There could be a lack of support. As I mentioned in the previous chapter to this section, the blueprint of a sales champion model is not a termination justification. It is, rather, an instrument by which you can gain extensive knowledge about an individual salesperson's probability to perform well in a sales role and allow you to make informed decisions about how to proceed. The Blueprint of a Sales Champion model may confirm all your field evidence about a salesperson, but you might have a sales champion on your team and not realize it.

First, let's take a look at the hazards to keeping a poor performer who does, in fact, have a less-than-desirable profile. By this I mean a salesperson who has one or more conflicts with what the position requires. The conflict can be any combination of behavior style, values structure, or cognitive structure. Remember that of the four components of the Blueprint of a Sales Champion model, selling skills is the only area that can most easily be changed.

The fundamental hazard in keeping a poor sales performer is that you'll invest a great deal of time, energy, and money for very little or no return. A salesperson who doesn't have the capacity to go out and sell on a consistent basis requires a lot of attention from you, the sales leader. When the salesperson eats up your time, money, and effort, other problems begin to surface. The objective of any business is to get a return on its investment, and keeping salespeople who don't perform up to standards ends up not offering any value for their employment and causing serious problems within the company.

The results of that large investment in a non-performer become evident in a variety of ways. First, the low-performing salesperson's territory doesn't generate the revenue it should. Let me illustrate this with a case study.

Bill was an industry veteran. He had been with the company for years and had extensive product knowledge. He made $300,000 a year in personal income, and he brought in $1.4 million in revenue annually. The problem was that he was in a $10 million territory. We assessed his behavior, values, cognitive structure, and selling skills against the Blueprint of a Sales Champion model, and it was a clear mismatch. But because he had been with the company for so long, the sales manager didn't do anything. There was no accountability for Bill, and at the same time the company was struggling to compete. Bill's pay plan was too rich, so he didn't have to exert himself to satisfy his financial needs. The sales manager avoided difficult situations, and it affected the company's morale and bottom line significantly.

A mediocre performer in an important territory like this leads to severe problems. Leaving Bill in his current role was costing the company almost $9 million a year in lost revenues, regardless of his years of service and product knowledge, not to mention the opportunities for up-sell and referrals. Basically, the company was being held hostage by the sales manager's unwillingness to confront this problem and deal effectively with this mediocre performer. The principle here is pretty simple: If the inmates are running your asylum, you have no one to blame but yourself.

Another typical pitfall sales leaders encounter when keeping a poor performer is the loss of credibility. Spending considerable time trying to develop or train a low producer makes the sales manager look bad to the rest of the team. Devoting more time to a poor performer to bring him or her up to an acceptable level demonstrates to your best salespeople that they aren't as important. A sales manager who is always meeting with the last-place finishers and sending them to seminars and babying them along cause much more damage in the long run. Bottom line: You've got to know who is a player, who isn't, and which ones to invest in. Competition is too fierce to waste time on non-performers who either can't or won't deliver.

In addition to the sales manager's loss of credibility, keeping a non-performer too long kills morale among the stronger performers. It is very difficult for a salesperson to consistently deliver results when the sales manager does not invest time in him or her. When a sales manager spends the majority of his or her time attempting to fix the non-performers, the best salespeople can get discouraged. Obviously, when the best salespeople get demoralized by the sales manger, their performance can begin to slide. The prevailing thought becomes one of indifference and apathy, which ultimately leads to even more trouble for the sales leadership.

When a sales leader invests time and money into lower performers (those who do not have the capacity to perform) through incentives, changes to that salesperson's role, additional support, and so on, the result will typically not make the kind of difference necessary. What it actually does is reinforce bad behavior. When a salesperson sees that there is no accountability for lack of results, he or she will continue to engage in the same unproductive activities. When a sales leader does not address problems like this, it sends a strong message to the underachiever that the lack of accountability means his or her job is relatively safe. Instead of the salesperson striving to achieve higher levels of performance, the opposite will actually happen. Other salespeople will begin to see that they can do less and still hold on to their jobs. The sales leader ends up with a mutiny of sorts, and he or she has an uphill battle to attempt to alter the course.

A low performer who has no accountability from sales leadership can actually get a false sense of accomplishment. Because no one is coaching him or her on ways to improve sales numbers, he or she may believe he or she is doing a great job. Consider this example. Tom was the #1 salesperson at his company. The sales manager would take Tom with him when he called on very large and important accounts. The sales manager would land the account, then he'd hand that account over to Tom. Then, Tom would take all the credit for the account, but it was the sales manager who did all the work. Tom was more of a secretary to the sales manager during the sales process. It was up to the sales manager to actually bring in the new business.

Tom felt like he was doing exactly what he should be doing, and because he was consistently at the top of the sales team, he felt no need to change. The actions of the sales manager reinforced an inaccurate mindset about Tom's ability to perform. What was really the salesperson's responsibility (generating new business) was being handled by the manager. Without the efforts of his manager to go out and bring the new accounts in, Tom would have not ever reached the status he enjoyed as #1 salesperson. Do you do this, too? Do you land the majority of the deals or save your salespeople in the middle of a sales call?

The hardship many sales leaders face when it comes to a poor performer is not acknowledging that one salesperson performs less than another. That part is obvious. All you have to do is look at the monthly totals to see how much each salesperson sold. Knowing what to do with that lower performer is difficult. The Blueprint of a Sales Champion model provides detailed information on each salesperson's probability to sell, and it shows what areas within the sales process are strong and which ones need development.

Mediocrity is sometimes a function of circumstance. Too many sales managers complain about the nonperformance of their salespeople and waste precious time attempting to fix the problem with solutions that don't address the real underlying issues. Understanding why a salesperson performs at a mediocre level is much more valuable to you as a sales leader than simply assuming that the person is just an average individual. Let's look at two examples in which two sales managers had the same complaint about one of their salespeople and what the very different outcomes were.

Thomas, the sales manager, was ready to terminate Greg. Greg had been through all the company training and had been with the organization for nine months. In that time, he had never performed up to Thomas's expectations. Before letting Greg go, Thomas decided to evaluate him against the Blueprint of a Sales Champion model. Greg agreed. The results showed that Greg had a very poor cognitive structure. Many factors (such as goal-directedness, results orientation, commitment to selling, enjoyment of selling, handling rejection, and handling stress) he did not see clearly.

Thomas already knew that Greg had not delivered, but he didn't know why. After an explanation of the results, Thomas asked if Greg should have ever been hired. From what we uncovered, there was no way that Greg would ever have managed to become the kind of salesperson Thomas needed. Greg agreed that he needed to look for another position due to his nonperformance. In this case, Thomas had plenty to go on from the evidence he had collected through the nine months of employment and the evaluation confirmed it.

Unfortunately, the direct costs the company incurred for

keeping this low performer were approximately $70,000. However, the greatest costs were from lost sales opportunities and sales management time, which could not be recovered.

What did we learn? We learned that identifying the capacities of a sales candidate during the hiring process will weed out what appear on the surface as excellent salespeople. In reality, they aren't, but you now don't have to wait nine months or waste $70,000 to find out. That's the real payoff with the Blueprint of a Sales Champion model.

Now, let's look at another example. Rhonda was hired twelve months ago and was thirty days away from termination. The sales manager, Steve, was tired of trying to get Rhonda up to speed. Rhonda had gone through extensive training and shadowed other top salespeople, but Steve still saw poor results.

I asked if I could evaluate Rhonda against the Blueprint of a Sales Champion model before that thirty-day period was over to determine if termination was the best choice in this situation. Steve agreed. The results clearly showed that Rhonda had the ideal profile for the position. All four components of the model were in line with the sales champion profile. Steve was confused and skeptical that Rhonda's observable performance did not match the profile.

I shifted the focus from the nonperforming salesperson to Steve, the sales manager, and asked him a few simple questions:

- Does Rhonda have adequate product knowledge?

- How often are you riding along with Rhonda on sales calls and observing her in the field?

- What are Rhonda's sources of motivation?

I discovered that Steve did not have a good idea about what Rhonda knew and didn't know about their products and services. Yes, she'd been through the company's week-long training program. However, it hadn't been reinforced, and Rhonda was so caught up trying to get appointments that she didn't get grounded in many of the solutions that the company provided.

Next, Steve said that he rarely went out with Rhonda

because he was so caught up with putting out fires and dealing with paperwork. Besides, he sent Rhonda along with Robert, their top salesperson, to watch him sell during his first few weeks on the job.

Finally, he assumed that the compensation plan was adequate for a rookie salesperson. But in reality, he didn't quite know what a person's sources of motivation were. He thought all salespeople were motivated by money and that was all.

I explained to Steve that product knowledge is extremely important, but it's only part of the solution. The real key was riding along with Rhonda and observing her selling in a real-world situation. Think about it. Every NFL football coach works with his team every day. And then on Sunday, they're right there on the sidelines coaching them through every play of the game. Don't forget, the coaches, owner, and executive staff went through a long process and invested a lot of time and money to acquire the best players possible. Coaching and leading a sales team in this respect is no different.

Steve got the message. The recommendation was for him to take our sales management training to improve his management skills when working with Rhonda. He agreed. When he was fin-ished with the training, he decided to get Rhonda back into a follow-up class on product knowledge and have her work with some of the technical people to gain greater depth in the solutions offered. Next, he agreed to invest time in riding along with Rhonda to observe her in the field. I guaranteed him that he would immediately find some issues that were causing Rhonda not to succeed but that could be easily remedied. Our sales management training provided him a process for doing that. Finally, one of Rhonda's primary sources of motivation we discovered during the analysis was personal relationships. However, she had been left to her own devices after only two weeks and that made her feel completely isolated from the company. She didn't need to be stroked or her ego inflated, she just wanted a connection with the people she worked with. By spending time with Rhonda in the car on sales calls, Steve agreed that they would be able to develop a better relationship.

Within three months of Steve completing his sales management training and implementing the new strategies he learned, Rhonda became the #1 performer in her office. By the end of the year, Rhonda won the annual sales award for the entire company and exceeded her sales quota by 300%! The following year Rhonda again set the pace and was on target to repeat his performance.

What did we learn? A sales champion poorly managed will yield the same results as a poor performer.

It is so important to identify what is underneath the surface when it comes to a mediocre performer. You may have been in a similar situation as these two sales managers. By merely observing what is on the outside, you'll never know the true reason for success or failure. By making decisions based solely on what you see, you put yourself in a precarious position to make a choice, but will you make the right one? Assuming that a salesperson is not performing because he or she is simply not good at what he or she does can be detrimental to the overall success of your company. Knowing why a salesperson is not performing to your expectations gives you much more to base that decision on, even if it ultimately is to let that person go.

When you know why someone performs well in your company, you can repeat that in others. You put yourself in a position to characterize exactly what qualities are necessary in your specific industry, organization, and individual sales roles. By having a repeatable system for hiring and developing a sales team, you end up with a better long-term positive result.

Not every situation will end up being a choice of firing an employee. The lack of results you see in a particular salesperson may simply mean he or she is not the right person for a sales position in your organization but could easily be excellent in another role. Valuable people who just aren't good at sales can many times be placed in another position that allows them to perform remarkably well. By considering the option of changing someone's position, you retain that person's knowledge of the company or the product or service, expertise in strategic analysis, or any number of other qualities. Many times a mediocre salesperson with extensive knowledge about the product makes an excellent marketing professional, trainer, customer service representative, or even sales manager.

It could also mean that the management strategies need to be reevaluated and new practices put into place like we did with Steve. Using the Blueprint of a Sales Champion model can aid you in the development of an untapped sales superstar.

The key with mediocrity is defining why someone performs poorly within a role. A quarterback will almost always make a poor offensive lineman. If you put him in that position, he's most likely to fail. He's still a great quarterback, regardless of his current role. The simple fact is that he shouldn't be an offensive lineman. The same goes with salespeople. Knowing what characteristics make a great salesperson allows you to use that knowledge to build a great sales team.

It's definitely true that a square peg won't fit in a round hole, but you just have to make sure that the peg is truly square. You have to know why it seems square, and you have to make sure when you hammer it into the round hole, you're doing so with the right tools. A butter knife isn't going to help. A sledgehammer may be unnecessary. Maybe the peg is actually round, but unless you test it thoroughly, you'll never know. The risk involved in forcing the wrong person into a sales role is as high as discounting a truly excellent performer for the wrong reasons. Finding the source of a salesperson's performance (good or bad) gives you a much better chance of successfully managing him or her and the rest of your team.

As I've said several times, the Blueprint of a Sales Champion model doesn't work in a vacuum. The connection between the sales manager, the capacities of your sales candidate or existing team member, and their results from the blueprint model are all extremely important. The next chapter shows you what the sales leader's role is and how to maximize the blueprint within the context of the entire sales team.

10

IF YOUR HEAD HURTS, QUIT BANGING IT AGAINST THE WALL

The role of the sales leader is often inaccurately defined. Many times it seems like nothing you do works with any consistency. One day with one salesperson your brilliant management tactic works, but then the next day with another salesperson, it offers no relief to your ongoing aggravation with low performance. Knowing what strategies work with every salesperson can ease that pounding in your head when you feel like you getting nowhere with your team.

By now, you know there is much more to salespeople than meets the eye. You may have even had some notion that this was true anyway, but you never had a good handle on it. Just because you have the information on hand doesn't mean you'll have great salespeople. The role of the sales leader is one of the toughest jobs around. Not only do you have to stay informed about emerging trends, new competitors, and bottom lines, you have a host of unique salespeople to monitor and develop.

Watching your company's highs and lows on paper may be a whole lot easier than actually determining what makes them occur. But having an accurate and comprehensive assessment of why each salesperson performs the way he or she does gives you a tremendous advantage in creating a repeatable formula for success. This fact is really the key to making your job easier, more enjoyable, and less stressful. When you have a thorough analysis of how, why, and when each salesperson will perform at maximum capacity, it allows you to build a well-oiled machine for producing excellent results on a regular basis. Otherwise, how will you really ever know *why* you have top performers, mediocre performers, and poor performers? How will you know why your turnover rate is so high? How will you know *why* sales are low?

The root causes for both success and failure lie in each salesperson and how well the sales leader can capitalize on the individual make-up of the team. Any team has to have a leader who knows each member's strengths and weaknesses to make good decisions. Imagine a construction foreman standing on the curb of a newly graded lot with all of his subcontractors and he says, "Okay, get to work. Let's build a house we can all be proud of," and then drives off. The resulting structure might resemble a house, but would it be livable? Would it not be a more solid construction if the foreman stayed on site and watched the house being built every day and address issues as they came up, rather than attempting to fix the foundation after the shingles were on the roof? Of course!

This kind of constant observation of the individuals on your sales team allows you to keep a better working knowledge of how to lead them to create the best possible outcomes. You know you have to observe your sales team to make good choices, but how do you answer those nagging questions that pop up all the time? Why does he do that? How can she discount every sale? Why won't he make more calls? Why won't she follow up and follow through? Why aren't they motivated? Why can't they sell more?

A sales leader must be able to set the vision for the sales team. Without doing this, you will never have a truly strong team. You must forge the culture. You have to know what the vision is, establish the vision, communicate the vision, live by the vision, and implement strategies to fulfill the vision. This fact is first and foremost the role of the sales leader. A company with a cloudy vision will suffer from short-sighted decisions. When you have limited visibility, all you can see is what is directly in front of your face. But when the vision is clearly thought out by you and explained to your team, you have a much greater chance for success.

To fully integrate that vision to your team, you have to know them. You have to know them beyond what their monthly report totals show. Every single salesperson on your team is unique. You have to use this to your advantage. I have three children who have different personalities, unique drivers, and specific talents. If I tried to raise them using the exact same methods, I would get very different results. Having only one method of dealing with all your salespeople is like having multiple children with a wide range of personality characteristics and trying to teach them exactly the same way. The rules of our house remain the same regardless, but how my wife and I deal with each child depends on their personal make-up. What works with one child doesn't necessarily work with another. If you have children, you know what I mean. I know my children very well, and because you obviously haven't known your salespeople from birth, you must do everything possible to get to know them both externally and internally. Without having a grasp of both aspects of a salesperson's make-up, there's really no way you can effectively lead them in a manner that creates the right situation for them to grow and develop.

Once you understand them on a deeper level, it is imperative to avoid the temptation to simply manage your team. Within a sales team, you should spend more of your time *coaching* instead of managing. This is where many sales leaders miss the mark. They spend a considerable amount of time managing a group of people they have relatively little information about. Many times they manage around the same problems that continually arise or are busy putting out fires instead of implementing proactive strategies that deliver acceptable sales results. Assuming the duties of a coach means leading by example, working with your players often, and supporting their efforts when needed. A sales leader needs to be aware of each team member and how to develop him or her to achieve the best possible outcome. A manager watches, waits, and reprimands; a coach observes, provides hands-on instruction, role models, offers advisement, and creates a positive environment for improvement. Notice the level of engagement the coach has as opposed to the manager. Which one are you? Are you observing, coaching, providing feedback, and developing your salespeople or are you managing from behind a desk?

Finally, the role of the sales leader is to make decisions that are in line with the overall goals of the company. Sometimes those decisions are difficult. You have to decide which salesperson is right for a particular territory. You have to hold poor performers accountable. You have to determine exactly what kind of training is needed for improvement. The complex sales process is multi-faceted, and every salesperson has varying degrees of competence in each area. If you were building a house and the bricklayer just wasn't doing a good enough job of estimating the number of bricks to use, you wouldn't train him on how to mix mortar. You'd teach him estimating skills. The same goes for salespeople. If you have a weak closer, why train her on networking if she can walk into a room and immediately strike up a conversation with anyone?

Making these tough decisions is part of your job as sales leader, but isn't it a little ridiculous to assume you can make those decisions based on limited sources of information? Does it make sense to choose a certain action when you're not really sure of the source of the problem? Whether it's the ultimate decision to terminate a salesperson or just deciding on the type of training needed, with only partial data gathered from observation and sales reports, it's easy to misdiagnose the problem, which only leads to more headaches and frustration.

These four characteristics of sales leadership–setting the vision, knowing the team, coaching the team, and making clear decisions–are necessary for the success of your team. It may seem obvious that you need to perform these functions, but many times sales leaders don't achieve their objectives simply because they lack the information necessary to do them. The blueprint of a sales champion model offers the information you've been looking for. Although it cannot assist you in setting up that vision for the company, it can greatly assist you in the other three areas. Let's look at each of them.

Know Your Team

Socrates said it best when he said, "Know thyself." As a sales leader, you must know who you are and who works for you. Relying on numbers from reports isn't quite enough data to go on. The Blueprint of a Sales Champion model provides the extra information that field observations cannot offer. Many times the philosophies the sales leader brings to the position contradict the objectives he or she wants to fulfill. Let's take a look at another scenario that explains this concept.

Frank was the sales manager with a dozen salespeople under him. He was a very personable guy who wanted to be friends with each of his staff members. He wanted to connect with them and engage them. He was happiest when a salesperson wanted his opinion or advice. Rick's Blueprint of a Sales Champion model showed a Doer/Talker behavior profile and values profile with high Political and Economic scores. Rick wanted to run his own show and make as much money as possible. He enjoyed taking control of his territory and mostly wanted to be left alone to do so. Frank's sales management style seemed too intrusive and personal to Rick. He felt like he was being watched too closely and micromanaged. He didn't want to go to lunch or talk about his weekend plans. He preferred the "stick to business" approach. His philosophy was, "Give me what I need, and I'll deliver results." He didn't mind engaging people, but he wanted to do it with those who could become clients.

Frank didn't realize that Rick didn't want to be friends with him. Rick liked Frank, but he just wasn't motivated by personal relationships with his co-workers or boss. This aspect of Rick isn't a bad thing by any means. It just shows that he wasn't wired that way. He wanted Frank to let him be more independent and autonomous. He wanted to be left alone and when he needed help, he'd ask for it. As a result of Rick's standoffish behavior, Frank felt like Rick was distant, unresponsive, and not acting like a team player. In reality, Frank simply did not know Rick's unique sources of motivation and was pushing the wrong buttons in an attempt to get the best results out of him. This thought process was based on what Frank would be motivated by, not Rick. Had he discovered the ideal environment for Rick and how he would like to have been managed using the Blueprint of a Sales Champion model, Frank would have had a top performer working for him. Instead, his own ideas got in the way, and Rick eventually left.

Harry, another salesperson on Frank's team, had a strong motivation for forming personal relationships with his co-workers and clients, as well as a very strong Talker behavior profile. He loved connecting with both prospects and peers. He and Frank often had long conversations about tactics, strategies, and prospects, as well as home life and sports. Both Harry and Frank were motivated by the same thing-the need to form personal relationships with co-workers.

Harry and Rick both had extremely good qualities that allowed them to generate business, but because Frank didn't realize some of the internal components of both salespeople, he often felt like Harry was a better salesperson than Rick. The reality is that Frank's own philosophies about his management style had more to do with assumptions than the actual performance of the salespeople. When he realized that Rick was simply motivated by something other than relating to people, he realized that he could relate to him much better. Unfortunately, he found this out too late.

Using the Blueprint of a Sales Champion model to know your salespeople better gives you the ability to alter your approach to various salespeople on your team. If you as the sales leader don't know yourself, you can never expect your salespeople to take the initiative to understand themselves better. It is always best to lead by example, so having your own blueprint gives you useful tools to understand your strengths and weaknesses when you interact with your team. When Frank recognized that he was motivated by the interaction with others and his desire to connect with them, he realized that some of his salespeople appreciated that approach, whereas others did not. Once he was aware of this difference, he was able to be more objective in assessing each salesperson's performance and then tailor his approach accordingly.

Coach Your Team

Knowing each of your salespeople with the aid of the Blueprint of a Sales Champion model gives you a much more targeted approach when it comes to coaching them. Many sales leaders are trying to improve salespeople with the ineffective methods. The blueprint model specifically tells you inside the sales process what the strengths and developmental areas are across multiple measurements, internally and externally, for every salesperson. When a sales leader attempts to address a salesperson's lack of ability to perform without knowing exactly what the problem is, time and money typically are wasted.

What a lot of sales leaders do is look at the aftereffects of a slow month and assume that the salespeople are not doing a good job. The blueprint model is not restricted by the boundaries of a monthly time frame. Coincidental ups and downs are irrelevant to a top-performing salesperson's ability to sell. A salesperson who has poor prospecting skills will have poor prospecting skills every month-even when he or she gets lucky and a big one falls in his or her lap. A salesperson who can't handle rejection won't handle it better if he or she breaks a record one month.

What the Blueprint of a Sales Champion model does for you as a sales leader is show you exactly which areas of your salesperson needs development. One salesperson might need to learn better questions to ask or how to handle stress more effectively, and another might improve through understanding different behavior styles and how to modify his or her own to gain more trust with prospects.

For example, Carol was expected to generate most of her own leads. She was brilliant at networking. She met prospects with a warm, genial manner, yet she didn't close nearly as many sales as she was supposed to. Her sales manager was baffled by what he thought should have been the best salesperson on the team. Every month Carol made more calls than was expected. When the sales manager assessed Carol against the blueprint model, he realized that she had a strong Doer/Talker style, which was the reason she looked so much like a top salesperson-very high energy, persuasive, charming, and aggressive. However, on a cognitive level, Carol did not see clearly the attributes required for success in the needs analysis step of the sales process.

Carol's problem was that she was a poor listener and lacked

confidence in herself and in her role-despite her type A personality. She didn't ask nearly enough questions to determine the needs of her prospects. When she did go to finalize the sale, she was attempting to close on much less information (and much less trust) than if she had asked more questions and been more confident during the process. When she failed to make a sale, the cause was the same every time. Though she was great at getting in the door, she was too eager to have the prospect sign on the dotted line. Her lack of confidence and attentive listening prevented her from asking the tough questions and finding out enough information about each prospect's issues, which led her to perform below her sales manager's expectations.

Fortunately, Carol's sales manager called me and asked that I assess her against the Blueprint of a Sales Champion model. Instead of making a wrong assumption about Carol's ability to sell at all, he realized that her area for development lay in improving her listening and confidence-building attributes. Carol wouldn't respond very well to lengthy seminars on how to ask better questions, so we provided her feedback on what we saw and then coached her in small segments on self-awareness, listening skills, and confidence-building strategies. The sales manager took the detailed information from our results to help Carol increase the number of sales she was able to close. After the coaching sessions, Carol's close rate increased significantly.

The sales manager invested time and resources wisely. He based his coaching on objective feedback he received from us about Carol's specific areas of development. Carol was happy with the method used to coach her because it was targeted to her specific area of development, and the sales manager was happy that Carol was finally reaching her goals. Had the sales manager used a different strategy that didn't account for Carol's unique areas of development, the results may not have been as helpful to Carol or the company.

Making the right choices when it comes to a salesperson's developmental needs can make the difference between improvement or continued low performance. By using the Blueprint of a Sales Champion model, you avoid the loss of time and money from inaccurate or misapplied training.

Making Tough Decisions

The hardest part of being a sales leader is trying to make the right decisions that will fit in line with what's best for the company and your salespeople. The challenge many sales leaders face is often done without resources sophisticated enough to ascertain if a sales candidate will or won't perform or why an existing one doesn't. Without knowing the root causes for success and failure, any choice that's made is somewhat tenuous and risky. What may look like the best answer can easily backfire in unforeseen ways. The Blueprint of a Sales Champion model is comprehensive enough to allow you to see the whole picture without blinders. The question is this: Is the salesperson salvageable or not? Most decisions you have to make about a salesperson boil down to this simple fact. Is he or she worth keeping? If the answer is yes, then the blueprint model gives you specific direction on what to do to develop the person. If the answer is no, then your evidence will be confirmed by the model. Either way you won't truly know if you're making the right decision without having the complete picture of the salesperson.

Recall the two case studies from the previous chapter: one salesperson that really was not a good fit for the position and one that looked like a mismatch but was actually a sales champion. Both situations turned out for the best, but without the Blueprint of a Sales Champion model, the outcomes would have been based on only partial information.

When you use the blueprint model to help you make decisions, not only does it make it easier for that individual case, it also helps build a reliable and repeatable system for future hiring and coaching choices. Instead of making a single decision about one salesperson, with the blueprint you can foresee problems before they happen again. Consider the following example.

William had to terminate a salesperson for unethical behavior. Before leaving, William requested that the salesperson be evaluated against the Blueprint of a Sales Champion model. The results showed that this salesperson had a very low Regulatory score on the values profile, which means that he didn't place a lot of value on rules, codes, or policies. The salesperson had a great interview, and William really liked him a lot. Eager to get the position filled, he hired him, but several months into his employment, William noticed that the salesperson never wanted to follow the rules. William was constantly making apologies and counseling him on what to do and not do. This maverick mentality created quite a problem, and finally William had no other choice than to let him go.

Armed with the knowledge of the Blueprint of a Sales Champion model regarding individuals with low Regulatory scores, William set out to fill the position again. This time he evaluated all five of the candidates using the blueprint model prior to offering a job. Each candidate had the Doer/Talker behavior profile, but two of them scored extremely low on the Regulatory value. Even though he liked both of them very well and after the initial interview felt like they were close to being his top picks, he chose to investigate further before making his decision. Without hesitation, William made the decision that would be best for the company in the long run than just going purely from the interview. If he hadn't used his previous experience with the blueprint, he would have never known what traits to avoid, and the likelihood of another disastrous salesperson would have been greater.

Again, the blueprint model is one-third of the hiring process, used in conjunction with the background check and the interview. Each of these three is significant because each part will provide information that the others don't. The background will tell you what the interview and the blueprint model won't. The interview will reveal information you can't learn from the background or the blueprint. Finally, the blueprint will tell you things that the other two won't. Be sure to use all three of these to acquire as much information as you can to make the best possible hiring decision.

Sales leaders will always have tough decisions to make, but there's no reason to make them alone when the powerful

Blueprint of a Sales Champion model can provide insight and help you avoid making costly mistakes. Whether it's a decision regarding hiring or one involving an existing employee, using this model to guide you in those decisions gives you a greater probability to sticking to your overall vision for the company, as well as gives you benchmarks for what kind of people you need to have on your team.

The role of the sales leader is very simple in theory, but it's much harder in reality. When something comes along that assists you in that role, it only makes sense to take advantage of it. Otherwise, you'll end up endlessly banging your head against the wall trying to figure out why nothing ever works out the way you want it to.

CHAPTER 11

FIXER-UPPERS: WHAT TO DO WITH EXISTING SALESPEOPLE

One of the biggest questions facing sales leaders has always been simple yet emphatic: "What do I do with the ones I have?" As a sales leader, it is your job to maximize performance in each salesperson on your team. The problem is that a one-size solution doesn't fit all. The fact that every member of your team is an individual and unique makes it necessary to develop specific methods for fixing sales problems with team members.

Most sales leaders have a good idea who the top performers and who the worst performers are. It's usually the group in the middle that fall into the category of marginal. They have performed at an adequate level, yet you wish they would do just a little bit more. You know they could bring in more business, but you haven't focused on what it will take to get those results.

I recommend individual, personalized development plans based on the results of the Blueprint of a Sales Champion model. Because the blueprint is a comprehensive evaluation that measures more than just skills and behavior, you can determine why a salesperson may not be performing and how to go about resolving the issue.

Though it is true that not all salespeople should be in a sales role, we'll save the issue of termination for a later chapter. What you're more concerned with is how to generate higher sales, bigger margins, stronger prospectors, consistent closers, and low turnover with the sales team you currently have. Even though salespeople each have their own strengths and areas for development, I want to show you the biggest issues salespeople face and what can be done about them.

As I've mentioned before, selling skills is an area that can be taught. If a salesperson is weak in asking the right questions, then skills training on asking good questions can prove useful. The same applies to any other area of selling skills. The problem more salespeople face does not pertain to selling skills but instead revolves around things like behavior conflicts, a lack of clarity in cognitive structure, or a values conflict with the role. Issues in these areas are not so easily remedied.

Interactive Inflexibility: A Behavior Conflict

We'll begin with the behavior conflict I see most often among salespeople. It may sound a little New Age at first, but the practical application of self-awareness has far-reaching effects. Self-awareness is a critical key to getting more things done in less time regardless of the salesperson's behavior style. Interactive *in*flexibility, or lack of self-awareness, is an obstacle a salesperson can overcome, as long as he or she is willing to learn and has the necessary tools to help.

The problem many salespeople face is that they have no idea what behavior styles are in the first place. By not knowing that behavior styles exist and are definable and measurable, they have no way of knowing their own or those of the people to whom they're trying to sell. Finally, having no definitive knowledge of the four behavior styles (discussed in Chapter 2) provides them no way to modify their behavior when dealing with different kinds of prospects, clients, and co-workers.

For example, a salesperson with a Doer behavior style attempts to sell to a prospect with the Controller behavior style. Without some modification on the salesperson's part, the result can be disastrous. The Doer is high energy, bottom-line-oriented, and aggressive, and the Controller is low-energy, detail-oriented, and reserved. This salesperson can come across as intimidating, and the prospect will become critical or quietly refuse to buy. Behaviorally, a Doer and a Controller have the least common ground on which to meet each other. The aggressive salesperson has a much better chance of getting a positive response from reserved buyer when he or she modifies his or her behavior style by slowing down, paying more attention to details, and exhibiting patience.

The solution for interactive inflexibility is to understand what behavior styles are and how to use this information with every individual a salesperson comes in contact with. Without full knowledge of the four distinct behavior styles, a salesperson is really at a disadvantage before he or she ever picks up the phone and meets a prospect.

The sales leader, with the help of the Blueprint of a Sales Champion model, can determine each salesperson's behavior style and use that information to reconstruct previously unsuccessful sales attempts. When the basic components of each behavior style are explained, the sales leader and the salesperson can look at sales calls that did not end up in a closed sale and formulate specific reasons for the failure. The failure may have been due to a behavioral conflict between the salesperson and the prospect. Knowing that, successful solutions can be developed for gaining those kinds of prospects on future sales calls.

The Blueprint of a Sales Champion model details the salesperson's own behavior style. It shows him or her how he or she is most likely to act, and then he or she can begin recognizing other people's behavior style based on the characteristics of the four styles. Knowing one's own style and that of those one comes in contact with will help one modify one's style to the prospect, which results in a better rapport.

By modifying one's behavior style, a salesperson has a much better chance of meeting the prospect on their ground. Approaching a prospect in a non-threatening way is crucial. When meeting a prospect for the first time, a salesperson should not be high-energy or low-energy or formal or informal. By approaching in a neutral way, an immediate behavioral conflict with the prospect is prevented. Because you want your salespeople to have every advantage when selling, the last thing you want is to have excellent products and services but a salesperson who alienates half of his or her prospects because he or she thinks enthusiasm is the only way to sell. By approaching in neutral, this also allows the salesperson to gauge a prospect by tone, speech patterns, and body language. Then the salesperson can assess whether the prospect is inclined toward a detail-rich conversation or a get-to-the-point sales call and proceed from there.

When a sales leader can recognize that a salesperson's behavior style is the cause of missed sales opportunities, coaching that person on behavior style in general and how to use behavior style as an indicator of a prospect's own behavior characteristics can turn unsuccessful sales calls into buying clients.

The knowledge of behavior styles also works inside the company. There are many instances in which a sales leader has come to me wondering why the sales team gets along so poorly with the customer service or accounting departments. The fact that everyone has a unique behavior style means that understanding how to effectively engage each style can reduce tension and aggravation within an organization as well.

Successful salespeople who prospect for new business typically have behavior styles with high Doer and Talker styles, whereas customer service and accounting staff members are more likely to have high Pacer and Controller styles. When a salesperson needs to communicate with employees in other departments, they can use the knowledge of behavior styles to maximize their effectiveness and reduce conflict.

Instead of rushing in, spouting off a quick ramble of information, and expecting a lower-energy behavior style to assimilate all of it just as quickly, a salesperson can adjust his or her style to talk slower, provide lots of details in a rational order, and listen more carefully to the other person.

Years ago I worked with a nice woman in our own accounting department. She had a dominant Controller style, and I'm a Doer style. Our energy levels were completely opposite. We had communication problems from the start, and I alienated her without knowing it. When I would go into her office, I would stand over her desk and point to the items on her computer screen that I needed her to address. She didn't like that.

After I learned about behavior styles and how to modify my own, I developed a strategy to increase the effectiveness of our working relationship. I would enter her office and immediately sit down. Two things happened. First, my energy level went down and matched hers because I was sitting and relaxed. Next,

I wasn't looking down at her. Instead, we were eye to eye and now on an equal plane. This simple strategy worked wonders, and we got a lot more accomplished and had a very productive working relationship as a result. When I began applying this and other similar behavior modification strategies in the sales arena, the success followed.

This practical application in self-awareness, once defined and implemented, can help marginal salespeople achieve better results. Without the Blueprint of a Sales Champion model, you may continue to hear excuses from your salespeople about why another prospect failed to buy.

Handling Rejection: A Cognitive Issue

Handling rejection is a big issue that salespeople face. It's almost impossible to pick up on this in an interview. As a sales leader, you may have no idea that a salesperson's performance issue has anything to do with handling rejection. A salesperson with a Doer/Talker behavior style will look like the kind of person that is fearless when facing rejection, but in reality, these two things (behavior style and cognitive structure) are totally separate issues.

A salesperson who isn't performing at the necessary level may have this issue, but you may never be able to definitively point to it as the source of the problem through conventional observation. What will typically happen is you'll see more reluctance to make phone calls and initiate relationships with new prospects. Unfortunately, most sales managers never make the connection between their salesperson's failure and their fear of rejection because most of the time the salesperson projects confidence and enthusiasm. It's like their outside doesn't look like their inside.

This issue is very common among salespeople, and dealing with it as a sales leader can be difficult. Using the Blueprint of a Sales Champion model, you can determine whether a salesperson has an issue with rejection and may be able to coach him or her through it, depending on your willingness to invest in him or her, his or her willingness to be coached, and his or her overall capacity to perform. Unlike interactive inflexibility (where explaining behavior styles can greatly assist salespeople's understanding of an unknown concept), coaching a salesperson to avoid a negative emotional reaction to rejection is not so easy.

A salesperson who does not clearly see how to handle rejection may not develop an iron will where no amount of rejection bothers him or her, but as a sales leader, you can make him or her aware of the issue and to some extent help him or her manage around it. This idea of creating awareness is very important. Having the information from the Blueprint of a Sales Champion doesn't mean the sales leader can simply expose the salesperson to this area of development and see an immediate change. A person's clarity of thinking is not as malleable as modifying behavior style.

Even so, a salesperson who experiences a fear of rejection can work around it to perform the functions of the sales role. By having the blueprint, the sales leader can recognize that a lack of focus in handling rejection may be the reason for poor performance. What might have been misjudged as lack of motivation or some other corollary issue can be pinpointed directly to this specific challenge. That's worth a lot because now you've identified the problem and a targeted solution can be applied. No more guessing in the dark for a fix to an unknown problem.

Once the root cause for the poor performance has be identified, the sales leader can focus attention on asking questions related to the salesperson's failed attempts. By asking questions like, "How many rejections did you get today?" and "What went through your mind when your prospect said 'No?'" you can help the salesperson by addressing the major area of development.

When a salesperson can begin say to himself after a rejection, "It's not about me. It's just not a good fit," then he can begin to potentially work around the problem. Placing emphasis on the root cause of the poor performance allows the sales leader to provide useful and practical coaching solutions for salespeople, whatever the issue.

In addition to recognizing and addressing the issue of handling rejection, the sales leader can measure the degree to which the salesperson has been able to manage around the problem.

Hopefully, the salesperson who doesn't see handling rejection clearly will have made enough progress through awareness and discipline that it is no longer a detriment to his or her performance.

The main thing to keep in mind in using the Blueprint of a Sales Champion model to evaluate cognitive structure is that no single attribute can be isolated. The entire cognitive structure must be taken in context, as well as the other three components. Just because someone can see clearly the attribute of handling rejection doesn't mean he or she isn't a clear thinker overall. It simply means that particular attribute is more of a challenge to him or her than it is to others.

When the problem of handling rejection is coupled with other cognitive issues, the cumulative effect of not being able to see things clearly may prevent a poor performer from managing around the areas of weakness. Measuring your salesperson against the Blueprint of a Sales Champion will show each of the areas for development, so it becomes the sales leader's job to determine whether the value of the salesperson is worth the time and energy necessary to help him or her manage around the trouble spots. Sometimes it is worth it, and other times it's not.

Anything But Money And Influence: A Values Conflict

As you learned from the first section of this book, a sales champion typically has high Economic and Political values. The most pervasive problem I see in salespeople across a wide range of industries is a value conflict with the role. When a salesperson is not motivated by making money and influencing control, he or she will most likely not perform to a sales leader's expectation.

You cannot change your salesperson's value structure. As a sales leader and coach, you cannot make someone value money through training. A salesperson's values structure is firmly ingrained, and nothing you attempt to do will change this. Fortunately, you don't necessarily have to get rid of every salesperson who has a misalignment with values that the job rewards.

The Blueprint of a Sales Champion model provides this critical information about salespeople. Because values are deep-seated drivers, you'll never know what moves one salesperson to act and what moves another. You can use the blueprint as a guide to understand salespeople more clearly from a values standpoint.

When poor performance is a result of a values conflict, there are three choices a sales leader can make. First, you can keep the salesperson and change the external situation for him or her. For example, a salesperson may have a high Economic score, meaning he or she is motivated by making money, but the pay plan does not meet these requirements. An inappropriate pay plan can be too shallow or too rich and be a factor in preventing the sales-person from performing.

For instance, a salesperson is paid a fixed salary and is expected to sell as much as he can. Whether he sells 1 unit or 1,000 units, he'll still make the same. A salesperson with a high Economic score will not work as diligently to bring in more busi-ness because the motivation to make more money cannot be met. He or she has no control over his or her income.

The same is true when the pay plan is too rich. A client of mine offered a healthy base salary well into six figures. In addition to that high base salary, the salespeople could earn commissions above and beyond that, doubling their salary. Even with a high Economic value, the pay plan with the base salary that rich sat-isfied many of the salespeople's drives. Therefore, they lacked the drive to work toward the extra commissions. The company gave them too much carrot up front. We advised them to drop the base and keep the healthy commission as long as it was profitable for the company. They did and the non-performers weeded themselves out and the sales champions thrived.

In each of these cases, making alterations to the pay plan can change the way the sales leader looks at the sales team. In the first case, providing the salesperson with the opportunity for bonuses or incentives will allow him or her to generate the kind of money he or she is internally driven to want. In the second scenario, my suggestion was to lower the base salary to the point where the salespeople would not have their Economic values met solely by the regular paychecks, and the result was a clean-up of the sales team with the sales champions staying to reap the benefits of their efforts.

Though the values structure of the salespeople rarely changes (example: A salesperson typically won't change from high Economic to low Economic, except perhaps from a traumatic life event), the sales leadership can make specific adjustments that cater to the individual salesperson's drivers. By pinpointing the most important values a salesperson has through the use of the Blueprint of a Sales Champion model, sales leaders can keep existing salespeople. Not only do they retain them by using the blueprint as a guide to making decisions, those relatively minor changes in structure of the job can increase productivity, making the expense of the changes insignificant.

The second option you have regarding a values conflict is to keep the salesperson by changing his or her role. Without the high Economic and high Political value scores, a salesperson typically won't perform at a sales champion level, but he or she may be very valuable in other ways. An industry veteran who just isn't motivated by making money can function in a number of other capacities within a company and ultimately be happier and more productive.

A salesperson who has a strong drive to influence power and control but isn't so concerned about increasing wealth (low Economic, high Political) can be an excellent candidate in the training department. The ideal situation for an outside salesperson is the high Economic Value, but if an existing salesperson has a high Theoretical value instead of a high Economic value, he or she may be much more motivated to exercise influence through providing knowledge.

Placing this kind of person in a sales training role will allow the company to tap into the years of experience in a way that benefits revenue goals as well as satisfy the individual's personal goals. This is a win-win situation because the sales team gains a highly effective teacher, instead of keeping a poor performer.

Another example of a change in role is when a salesperson's blueprint shows a high Economic but low Political drive. This means that the salesperson is motivated by making money, but he or she isn't motivated by calling his or her own shots and being independent. For this kind of salesperson, a change from an outside prospector to an account manager that services existing accounts may allow the salesperson to perform exceedingly well. By dealing with existing accounts and building strong relationships, the person is still able to make the money desired, but not on his or her own. Account management and relationship building with existing accounts requires a less independent drive because the relationships are typically warm, not cold, and the salesperson has more of a routine and less ambiguity. The switch to account manager can give the company a strong player in the area of client relationship development without sacrificing new business because a salesperson isn't motivated by power and influence.

Once you have the Blueprint of a Sales Champion model for salespeople, you begin to see where the solutions lie. Making alterations in individual salespeople's jobs or placing them in different roles within the company takes a bit of creativity from the sales leader, but the benefits of retaining existing salespeople far exceed the negative aspects of turnover, especially when you have no idea what the problem is in the first place.

The last option for a salesperson with a values conflict is, in fact, to let them go. Sometimes there is no other option. The Blueprint of a Sales Champion model provides the clues for the conflict, but the decision to let a poor performer go is a combination of factors. In the end though, there are situations in which the values conflict between the individual and the role or the company culture do not merit keeping someone.

Even though it is usually more cost-effective to keep a salesperson you've made an investment in (if they can be turned around), a values conflict won't go away on its own. A salesperson with low Economic and low Political scores and high Theoretical and Aesthetic scores will most likely be motivated to act based on knowledge, beauty, and harmony. An existing salesperson with a values structure like this will have a very hard time performing to your expectations in prospecting-oriented sales role. He or she may also not fit into any role within the company, and the only viable option is to end the relationship. The key to determining if termination is the best choice is knowing whether the values that motivated the person can be used productively for the company. The Blueprint of a Sales Champion model helps sales leaders make that determination.

Deciding what to do with existing salespeople who aren't performing is really a crapshoot without understanding the entire situation. The problems of poor performance are very wide-ranging. Some salespeople can be "fixed up" to be more productive for the company, but others will never meet the standards.

Taking into consideration all of one's options when it comes to making decisions really can only be done with the help of a benchmark model like the Blueprint of a Sales Champion. Comparing your salespeople and candidates against the blueprint puts you as a sales leader infinitely more in control than basing decisions solely on observable behavior and previous work history.

Sales leaders want to have salespeople who perform exceptionally well. The costs of hiring, training, and developing those salespeople are high, so it's only logical to make those decisions based on all the components that make up the individuals. Employing the Blueprint of a Sales Champion model as part of the information-gathering and decision-making process greatly increases the chances that your fixer-uppers will be more valuable over time than simply having to offload them at a loss.

CHAPTER

12

THE BAD MEMORY FILE:
SALESPEOPLE YOU WISH YOU'D NEVER SEEN

For you, the "bad memory" file may be large. Even though you've told yourself a thousand times that you'll never hire another salesperson like that last one, you find yourself plagued with problem after problem when it comes to sales performance across the board.

I understand that many of the concepts in this book are abstract and somewhat difficult to convert into real life at first. Not only that, but the experience and the research behind the Blueprint of a Sales Champion model are pretty dense, too. As you read this chapter, think about salespeople you may currently have or ones you've had in the past. Unfortunately, you may recognize my descriptions all too well. The point I want you to see is that until now you may have recognized a salesperson's lack of performance but have not been able to label the root cause of the problem.

The characterizations of the following salespeople are rampant in today's sales society at all levels and in all industries. The solution lies in fully understanding why these salespeople are the way they are, not simply that they may not be such good players. I'm not going to explain what to do with these different kinds of people because making broad generalities doesn't solve problems. Training, development, and termination are options in each case, so it really depends on the individual and how he or she stacks up against the Blueprint of a Sales Champion when it comes to what to do.

The main thing I want you to see is that the salespeople for whom you have spent countless hours wondering why they fail have very specific reasons for why they under perform, and the reasons are measured and defined through the use of the

Blueprint of a Sales Champion model.

Behavior Problems

The Approval Seeker: Approval seekers want everyone to like them. They spend more of their time attempting to befriend prospects instead of developing trust. They want to engage and relate to their clients and prospects, so they attempt to sell based on the degree of that relationship they've established. What happens is that many people like them as a person, but they just buy more from those whom they trust.

The need to connect with others can be so important to Approval Seekers that it actually backfires on them. In the rush to shower a prospect with friendship and camaraderie, the opposite effect can occur. Prospects can be turned off by the inappropriate level of familiarity, which leads to disbelieving anything the salesperson might say about the product he or she is selling.

Approval Seekers typically have a very high Talker behavior style. Their intentions are genuine, but buyers aren't usually as interested in making friends when it comes to spending their money as much as they want to find someone whom they can trust to deliver. Because Approval Seekers are so insistent on being friendly, they can falter when their personal charm doesn't result in a sale.

This high Talker style can lead to a misunderstanding for

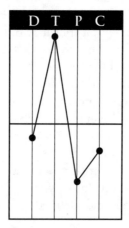

The Approval Seeker behavior style

salespeople. Their excuse for poor performance may be to claim that some prospects just don't allow for enough connection to develop for them to start selling. They spend so much of their time trying to figure out what to do to make the prospect like them that there's no time for anything else. Actually, the problem is an issue of interactive inflexibility and being able to understand a prospect's behavior style and act accordingly.

The Friendly Farmer: Friendly Farmers mostly want calm, stable waters. They don't enjoy chaos or change, and they're very concerned about image. Their favorite kinds of clients are ones that are already primed for buying. Prospecting for them comes too close to potential conflict, so they will try to avoid it if possible.

Friendly Farmers tend be very comfortable in environments where they know what to expect and can ensure that their actions are a positive reflection of themselves. Within the walls of the office setting, sitting across from an existing client at their favorite restaurant, and always being in familiar territory puts them at ease. Asking them to go out into the unknown world they can't control can be very taxing.

Friendly Farmers typically have a Talker/Pacer behavior style, instead of a Doer/Talker combination. They have a very engaging manner, and they like to accommodate others, but they only want to do this in a situation where they have a pretty good

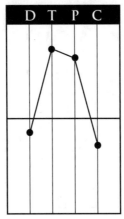

The Friendly Farmer behavior style

idea of the outcome. They are wonderful when it comes to servicing and supporting an existing client because that is their comfort zone.

The problem is that many sales organizations don't really desire salespeople who want to spend the majority of their time dealing with existing clients. There's no question that account management is important and there is a time to wear the farmer hat. However, prospecting can never stop.

The combination of Talker and Pacer behavior styles can be a tremendous asset to a company if the sales culture allows for it, but this behavior style can also be limited when required to continually discover and grow new customers.

The Turtle: Turtles have no sense of urgency. They do one thing completely before they move to another task. They are very methodical in their approach to getting things done, and when the need to juggle multiple tasks is important, they get frustrated at the lack of attention given to each part.

They will dot every "i" and cross every "t" if left to their own devices. For example, if they have to put a proposal together, they may spend three days making it perfect when it should have been done in a few hours. It's more important to take the time to do it right than it is to have it right now. They'll get their work done eventually, but in the meantime, new business is going to another company.

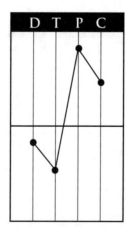

The Turtle behavior style

Turtles many times have the complete opposite behavior style from a sales champion. Turtles are typically Pacer/Controllers. Their energy level is very low, and they may look like they're never accomplishing anything fast enough. While others are quickly turning around new business, they will be content to attend to every detail, one prospect at a time.

If they are put in a situation where speed and urgency is imperative, Turtles will burn out quickly because they just don't have the necessary energy to keep up with that kind of pace. Plus their risk-aversion style can get crushed in a sales culture where one has to be quick on one's feet and deal with ambiguity to be ready for anything.

I once had a client who raved about one of his top performers. He asked that I run her through the blueprint model to see how she would fare. I noticed she had a Turtle behavior style, and he literally dropped the phone. He said, "Her lack of urgency is her greatest limiting factor. She does everything very well, but it just takes her way too long to get it done! How did you know?" I told him that even with a solid salesperson who values money and independence and is a clear thinker, a behavioral conflict with the role can prevent them from being a true sales champion. I recommended that if he wanted to keep her in a prospecting sales role, that he should consider sales support and/or a stronger marketing investment to help her acquire more leads and do less paperwork if those factors were slowing her down. If not, she would work much better in a "Farmer" role cultivating existing relationships where a sense of urgency is not required at the same level. He agreed and got busy working with her on how to best update her role in the company.

Not all situations will work out this well, but there is no doubt that a low-energy behavior style can prove to be a costly conflict between the Turtle and their sales role.

The Drill Sergeant: Drill Sergeants show no mercy. They are all about business. They're so much about business that they fail to recognize that they're ultimately selling to people. They can come across being very direct, overbearing, critical, and cold. Nothing appears to matter to them but the final goal of the sale, and whatever gets in the way will be trampled into dust.

In addition to being very straightforward, they're also quality-conscious. They want to get things done, but then they want to make sure it's the right thing to do. They can come across as being moody, and when they need to make a big decision, they have a hard time. They can look like a person with one foot on the gas and one on the brake, constantly starting and stopping.

Drill Sergeants are typically Doer/Controllers. They lack a people orientation. It's not that they don't like people—they just don't come across as warm and friendly, sometimes even when they try! They don't demonstrate a warm relationship at first. It typically doesn't come naturally to them. The Doer side is very aggressive, and the Controller side is very precise, so when the two styles come together, you have someone who comes across as a very rigid, serious, and direct salesperson.

They can cause difficulties with prospects, and they can also create a lot of conflict within your company. Their approach to engagement with other people can totally isolate and exclude the relational aspect of getting things done. In very extreme situations, they might even get into an argument with a prospect, all in the name of being right.

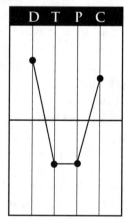

The Drill Sergeant behavior style

Cognitive Problems

The Dreamer: Dreamers always have great ideas. The problem is that they have difficulty implementing them. They are typically content to talk about pie-in-the-sky plans for the future that never materializes. The things they come up with may be wonderful concepts, but they fail to follow through to make them a reality.

Dreamers have the ability to see a goal or strategy or opportunity that others may not notice. They can be very enthusiastic in their delivery to their sales manager, but operational obstacles get in the way of the grand scheme, leaving the concept unfulfilled.

Goal-directedness is extremely important, but when being able to see the big picture is not coupled with tactical implementation, the whole process gets stalled. Dreamers are strong in the area of goal-directedness. Their problem is in results orientation. Without the ability to follow through with plans, Dreamers live in a world full of what might be, instead of what is.

This lack of clarity between getting from idea to reality makes Dreamers look good for a moment. When all they do is come up with ideas that they want someone else to implement, they lose credibility as a source of innovation through lack of initiative, which leads to ignoring the ideas they have in the future.

The Pinball: Pinballs are the opposite of dreamers. They are always busy. They tend to be involved in multiple projects at once. They get caught in the activity trap and are challenged to get anything done related to the overall goals and objectives of the company. They give the impression of being good salespeople because they're constantly busy.

That activity is misleading because they expend a lot of energy running around in circles. They don't get nearly as much done that applies to the overall company goals because everything they do is so disjointed and unfocused. It's like driving in the dark at high speed without the lights on.

Pinballs can have the behavior style of a sales champion but have low scores in goal-directedness. They can't see the big picture. They are content to stay busy working on activities that seem good to them, regardless of the importance they have in reaching their departmental or organizational goals.

The missing link here is the flip side of the Dreamers' problem. Pinballs rarely connect the dots between what they're doing and their goals. The inability to clearly see how things fit into the overall picture puts Pinballs in a position of working very hard to achieve very limited results.

The Cow: Cows need a cattle prod to get them going-and so do some salespeople. They may have the outward appearance of energetic go-getters, but every morning, they look around for an answer to the question, "What do I do today?" They wait to be told what to do and then have a difficult time getting started.

Cows will wait for directives from their sales leaders again and again. If they know they're supposed to go and meet new prospects, they want to know where to go first. If they know they're supposed to follow up with existing clients, they may want to know how to initiate the conversation. No matter what the situation, they always need for someone else to get them started.

The inability to clearly understand the concept of self-starting capacity can leave salespeople mired in questions. They look like they should have no problem with prospecting and generating new business from a behavior standpoint, yet they don't see that the responsibility for doing that on one's own is important.

Clarity of thinking from this standpoint is critical to the success of an outside salesperson. Not having the self-starting ability creates daily problems when Cows should be out in the field but are still hanging out in the barn.

The Excuse Maker: Excuse Makers don't clearly see where the root cause of a lost sale is. They spend their time complaining that the reason for their low sales volume is a result of the prospect, the product, the timing, the weather, and so on. They never make the connection between themselves and a lost sale.

Excuse Makers like to blame external elements for lack of results. When a sale doesn't close, they quickly have a reason ready for their sales managers. Instead of looking for answers and solutions for missed sales, they concoct stories in their minds, so they don't have to suggest that anything is their own fault.

Poor personal accountability is the issue here. When Excuse Makers fail to close a deal, they cannot see that they are the fundamental reason it failed, if they are responsible for it failing. They go to great lengths to avoid pointing the finger in their own direction. They just don't see themselves as the problem.

This inability to look within for reasons further complicates the problem because they look in every direction but the right one for an answer.

Values Problems

The Maverick. Mavericks see absolutely nothing wrong with making up the rules as they go along. One day they'll act one way, and the next day they may have changed their strategy. Do you have salespeople who don't want to play by your rules?

Mavericks can have a champion behavior style. They can be high-energy, direct, and outgoing, which was probably why they got hired in the first place. The reason Mavericks can act in such a counterproductive way has to do with their values. The Regulatory drive on the values profile tends to be very low.

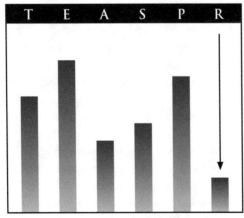

Profile with a low Regulatory level

T: Theoretical   S: Social
E: Economic   P: Political
A: Aesthetic   R: Regulatory

Mavericks may not value the rules, policies, or procedures that are part of your organization's philosophies. Variations of Mavericks are salespeople who have both the Regulatory and Theoretical scores very low. They may not want a set of rules applied to them, and they may not want to learn anything new.

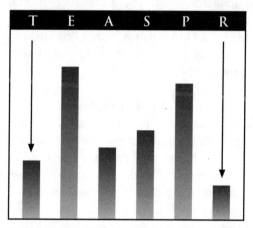

Profile with low Theoretical and Regulatory value

T: Theoretical   **S**: Social
E: Economic   **P**: Political
A: Aesthetic   **R**: Regulatory

This combination can make it very difficult for a sales manager to coach them. Again, this is not set in stone because there are exceptions to the rule, but I've seen it enough to know that this combination can frequently lead to heartache and frustration for you as it has done for others. As you well know, listening and learning are two keys to champion success in any field.

The Fundamentalist: Fundamentalists know exactly how everything should be done. They have a very rigid set of principles and procedures to conduct themselves through life and their careers. Very rarely can their sales managers tell them anything outside their personal code and have any effect.

Fundamentalists tend to have a solid metal frame built around them. When a new idea or technique is suggested to them, it's like taking a large sledgehammer and slamming it against their frame. It reverberates all through the structure, and Fundamentalists don't like this at all. They tend to take this stance: "I hear what you're saying, but I've got my own way of doing it."

I've seen that this inflexibility in not accepting new methods or ideas comes from a combination of low Theoretical and high Regulatory values. They see little value in learning new things because they either feel that they already possess the knowledge in the areas of their specific area of interest and they don't value venturing outside of it. The high Regulatory score shows they believe very strongly about a set of guidelines to live and work by.

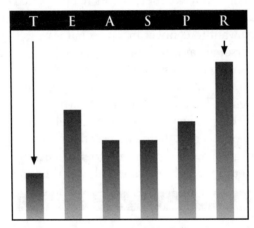

Profile with low Theoretical and high Regulatory values

T: Theoretical   S: Social
E: Economic   P: Political
A: Aesthetic   R: Regulatory

The conflict here is that the coachability factor can be very low. Even when Fundamentalists do not perform at the proper level, I've learned that it can be difficult for them to alter their personal set of rules to improve performance. Looking at most things as black-and-white issues doesn't allow them to work through the gray areas. When the Regulatory value is high, salespeople are so motivated by acting in accordance with their code they can fail to recognize the possibility of alternatives.

The Discounter: Years ago there was a commercial in which two friends were sitting together and one wants the other's drink. After having a heartfelt conversation, the one vying for the drink says with a sad face, "I love you, man." Do you have sales-people like this? They get so wrapped up in their prospect's or customer's pain that they become too emotionally tied into the other person. It can be a problem and here's why. They can lose sight of why they're there. When it comes to making the deal, they don't want to charge them for it or feel their price is too high. As a result, they frequently discount the price.

Discounters like to make their clients happy. The relationships they develop are more important to them than the money they make. They want to connect in a personal way, so they sacrifice their own personal gain, and that of the company, to ensure that the relationship remains strong.

Discounters can end up simply trading dollars and severely eroding margins. Their empathy turns to sympathy, and to justify the cost of the product or service they sell, they make it so appealing to buyers that there's no way they'd refuse. They tend to have very good relationships with their clients, but the cost of those relationships can be detrimental over the long run.

Profile with high Social value

T: Theoretical	**S**: Social
E: Economic	**P**: Political
A: Aesthetic	**R**: Regulatory

Discounters, who erode margins due to high levels of sympathy, typically have a high Social value.

They are so strongly motivated by sympathy that personal relationship building becomes the major force in working with them. Because they are more motivated by the cause to help others, they will take the lower price in favor of strong ties to the clients.

Discounters can be mild or severe, but a consistent discounter can cost a company significant revenue in lost sales. The Social score is important in selling because salespeople are dealing with people. But when it is too high, salespeople look for ways to deepen their relationships with prospects and clients, rather than increasing the company's bottom line.

These different types of salespeople have been simplified in these illustrations. There can be many other factors that affect someone's performance both long-term and short-term. They also represent just a small sample of some of the many issues related to poor performance. The combinations of behavior style, cognitive structure, values structure, and selling skills are all intermingled. The cause of poor performance usually isn't a single issue. Each of these areas of a salesperson's make-up works in tandem.

For example, a salesperson may have a cognitive issue with a lack of clarity in self-starting ability (the Cow) and have a values conflict (the Discounter) with the role. Or a salesperson may fit the description of a Dreamer and also have problems handling rejection.

There are many different types of salespeople in the world, so to truly know what a salesperson's obstacles are, the Blueprint of a Sales Champion model should be administered to find out. Many times what you as a sales leader think is the problem has very little to do with the real issue. Knowing how to dig deeper into why salespeople act the way they do, as well as investing the time and resources into do it, reveals a wealth of knowledge about how to handle the situation.

For so many sales leaders, it's not a question of determining if a salesperson has a problem. It's all about why he or she has that problem and what to do about it. That is one of the fundamental differences with the Blueprint of a Sales Champion model. It functions as a source for describing the salesperson, but it goes much further than that. It shows what can be done about it.

A blueprint is created to build things. We don't live in a world of only paper and ideas. Top sales performance is about engaging in the right activities. You must have a blueprint of your poor sales performer before you can decide if he or she can develop the necessary awareness and skills through the use of the sales champion model to achieve your expectations. Likewise, you won't know why your top performers are successful until you measure them against the model either. Defining a blueprint for your salespeople and candidates is the first step to building your ideal sales team. Just as you wouldn't start on a house without the plans, you can't build a sales team without a road map for success.

In the next chapter we will discuss how many times training seminars are a failed attempt at applying a skills solution to a people problem.

CHAPTER 13

THE INHERENT FLAW IN TRAINING SEMINARS

Who hasn't gone to a seminar to learn some new technique or strategy to become a better salesperson? How many times have you looked at the monthly numbers, knew something was wrong, and decided training was the answer? How many of your salespeople returned from a seminar pumped up with excitement only to discover two weeks, two months, and two years down the road that the same problems were occurring?

Training seminars have an unfortunate character flaw about them. In most cases the information presented is relevant, useful, and potentially helpful, but how can a couple of days of training change the entire direction of a salesperson's performance? What happens when the seminar is over? How does the salesperson retain and apply the knowledge he or she gained? What incentive is there to take the material from the conference hall to sales call?

The problem typically isn't the material presented at seminars and conferences. There is a dual issue. The first facet lies in the fact that our brains usually don't transfer information from the short-term to the long-term memory with only a single burst of exposure. Information will stay in the short-term memory banks for only a very short time if it is not consistently used and reinforced.

The second issue is that the material itself is not what the salesperson always needs. The salesperson can recognize the information as beneficial for growth, but he or she also has to see the value of *using* that information. If the salesperson isn't a good fit for the role to begin with, the skills training will never be fully implemented, no matter how well it was presented.

Consider this example. A sales manager, Keith, knew that his salesperson, Charles, had trouble prospecting for new business. Keith found a seminar coming to the area on prospecting techniques and signed Charles up for it. Charles went to the conference, and when he came back, he told Keith all about the new tools he learned for prospecting. So far, so good. Keith felt confident that Charles would start using these new tactics and become a better prospector.

Over the course of the following weeks, Keith closely monitored Charles's efforts in searching for new business. At first, Charles made additional phone calls, went to several networking events, and even moved along in the sales process with a couple of new leads. But by the end of the month, Charles had gone back to his regular methods, and new leads started dropping. When Keith confronted Charles about all the new techniques he'd learned and why he wasn't using them any longer, Charles said he just didn't think the new techniques worked for him.

Keith was a little irritated because the seminar hadn't been cheap, and in just one month, Charles was back to his old self, spending more of his time dealing with existing clients than looking for new ones. If Keith had given Charles the Blueprint of a Sales Champion model, he would have discovered that Charles had a cognitive challenge with handling rejection and a high value on knowledge.

Charles internalized the rejections he got, which made him become reluctant to call, yet he enjoyed the seminar because he valued knowledge for its own sake. In an effort to try to use the information, Charles held out for a while, but in the end, his inability to dealing with those prospects who said "no" was stronger than his ability to take the seminar material and use it. This is a classic case of cognitive and values structures impacting a salesperson's performance despite the actions of the sales manager. He knew how he should sell (i.e., use the prospecting skills) but his cognitive and value structure did not back up the behavioral characteristics necessary to perform.

Just because a salesperson knows the skills to use in a selling situation doesn't automatically mean those skills will be employed. This fact doesn't mean you should stop providing salespeople with training opportunities. On the contrary, most top salespeople want to gain additional knowledge to assist them in furthering their careers.

The lesson to be learned here is that seminars and conferences are mountaintop experiences. Eventually, salespeople have to come down to the valley of the real world where great theories and methodologies have to be implemented into daily action. If there is no follow-up, there will be no long-term gain. And if salespeople are the wrong fit in the first place, no amount of repetition or incentive will change their behavior.

So what do you do to avoid the costly expense of wasted seminars? Make sure that you've got the right salespeople first, and then train them.

14

TO FIRE OR NOT TO FIRE:
THE SALES LEADER'S NIGHTMARE

(Note: This section does not endorse termination decisions solely by the use of the Blueprint of a Sales Champion model or the tools used in the process. Termination, just like hiring, requires information from different sources and should not be considered on just the results of a profile.)

No matter how much you hate doing it; termination always seems to be part of a sales leader's life. For one reason or another, you find yourself faced with the tough decision of whether to let a salesperson go. Those reasons may have to do with poor prospecting skills, an inability to get in front of the decision maker or inappropriate activities.

Most sales leaders don't want to fire their salespeople. This doesn't come as a shock to you because you've been in that exact position, too. What you'd really like more than anything is for the salesperson to get it through his or her head what you want him or her to do and then just do it consistently. The problem is that there is a barrier between what you want the person to do and what he or she is actually doing. That barrier is why you are considering termination in the first place.

Most salespeople intend on doing a good job, but the reasons for their failure are wide-ranging. What you're faced with is knowing which decision to make—fire or not fire?

Unfortunately, most salespeople get fired because the sales leader based the decision solely on the results of the performance. The results of poor performance (low sales, low margins, lack of motivation, etc.) are not usually the cause of the problem. Making decisions based on observable data like monthly sales numbers don't always tell the whole story either. There's more to a salesperson's ability to function in the sales role besides him- or herself.

External forces that salespeople can't control, like market conditions, pay structure, sales manager relations, product flaws, poor customer service, bad press, and corporate culture, can all play a major part in why a salesperson isn't performing. Not knowing what the root cause of the problem is means that you may be letting your best salespeople go without even knowing it.

The Blueprint of a Sales Champion model helps you make those decisions more effectively. It gives you the reasons why a salesperson may not be reaching goals. It also may tell you that you have a sales champion on your hands, but there is something beyond his or her control that makes him or her underachieve.

We've already discussed the issue of how assumptions can be deceiving. Whether you have already made up your mind that a salesperson isn't going to work out or you're sitting on the fence about how to handle a less-than-ideal situation, failing to use our model can leave you in the dark about future decisions regarding low performers. And it puts you in a precarious position when it comes to explaining why the termination decision has been made. Having measurable data to back up your claims can be very beneficial when it comes to the face-to-face meeting with the salesperson you are going to terminate. However, the feedback you get on your salesperson from the Blueprint of a Sales Champion model is not the reason you would terminate him or her. It is there to help validate what you've already observed in the field–the person is not performing to your level of expectations.

How do you determine if termination is the right choice? You begin with the poor sales performer in question. What does he or she bring to the table? What do this person's results look like against the Blueprint of a Sales Champion model? Is there a behavior conflict? Is there a values conflict? Is the salesperson a clear thinker? Does the salesperson have the necessary selling skills?

Is the salesperson actually a sales champion but has a conflict with you, the sales leader? The would-be sales champion may be looking for more autonomy while you're micromanaging him. The salesperson will probably look unmotivated because he wants to be independent and take ownership of his territory, but you may be squelching that drive. A decision to fire this person may be just around the corner, but would it be the best thing to do? It may not.

Here's another example. The salesperson is high-energy, assertive, and always on the go. All of a sudden, her sales begin to drop off, and every prospect is buying from someone else. The economy is tight, and you're forced to cut the sales team. Because this salesperson has fallen to the bottom of the rankings among the rest of the team, you have to let her go. This could be a big mistake. The issue here is discovering what is going on in the marketplace. Are there new, lower-priced competitors? Has the company received some negative press about its product? The salesperson can't do anything about these kinds of things, but without understanding her make-up better, your decision is not based on all the facts. With the Blueprint of a Sales Champion model, you can see clearly that something outside the salesperson's control is the reason for the drop in performance.

Knowing the players on your team is the first step in deciding if termination is right. Once you've done that, the decision becomes infinitely easier. There are many times when your intuition is correct. What you see in the field is exactly what's in the Blueprint of a Sales Champion model. The benefit to validating your theories on a salesperson is that you have hard evidence to back up the decision.

Now, what if the blueprint shows a behavior or values conflict? Before I answer this question, I want to restate an important concept I've mentioned several times. The blueprint model should not be the sole method by which you make any decisions, hiring or firing. When the blueprint reveals that a salesperson has a serious conflict with the role, and it doesn't have anything to do with external forces, termination still may not be the best answer.

A salesperson with a behavior conflict might be a Friendly Farmer (Talker/Pacer behavior style). If you need prospectors, the Friendly Farmer can be a real drag on sales because he or she tends to want to deal with familiar territory. If the person is, in fact, really good at cultivating relationships with existing clients, a shift in job responsibilities may be the best course of action. By putting a Friendly Farmer into an account management position, where he or she can develop strong, deep relationships with existing clients, you retain the knowledge base he or she has without losing business in spite of the fact that this person is not geared toward making cold calls.

When the performance issue is related to a values conflict, the same method can be used. Is there another role within the company this person would be more suited for? For instance, if the salesperson had a low Economic but high Political and high Theoretical drive, a position in the training department might be ideal. The salesperson's desire for knowledge and control and influence can be channeled into teaching other salespeople product information, orienting new salespeople to the industry, and so on. The knowledge base and level of experience is irreplaceable even if the salesperson isn't motivated to make as much money as possible.

There are times, of course, when these options are not available, but without the Blueprint of a Sales Champion model, you'd never know that a salesperson just needs a little guidance and direction to become an outstanding player. Within the company goals, being creative and looking for ways to capitalize on the player you have already invested in can be an alternative to termination if the salesperson has the internal capacity to perform.

Unfortunately, there are salespeople who aren't sales champions in disguise or great players in the wrong role. Some salespeople just shouldn't be in sales. I've spoken to many salespeople who were in a situation in which they weren't performing. When I asked them why they were in sales, their response was typical. "My father was in sales. My brother was in sales." Or this classic, "Someone told me I had an outgoing personality, and I should go into sales." However, when I ask them if they wanted to be in sales, they admit that no one had ever asked them that, but in reality, the answer was no. Leaving the sales position ends up being beneficial for both the company and the individual. Without the commitment to selling or an innate enjoyment of selling, a conflict will eventually show up.

The benefit of the Blueprint of a Sales Champion model provides you with a more predictive means for evaluation. If a sales-person isn't performing at the level he or she should and there's an obvious conflict with the role, there is a very good chance that the behavior won't change. Without some kind of inter-vention, what you've seen in the past will be seen in the future. As a sales leader, you have to take that information as a piece of the puzzle that helps you make the best decision for the company.

What are some of the clues that show an existing salesperson is a bad fit? Does he or she contaminate the environment? Salespeople who constantly have something negative to say bring down an entire team. This negativity can come from a number of places, but when a salesperson is always complaining, you can bet that it affects the rest of your team. Having a chip on your shoulder and causing trouble is not worth dealing with–regardless of how they're performing. Other clues are unethical behavior, gossip, and generally being an all-around rotten apple.

The Blueprint of a Sales Champion model expedites this process. It doesn't mean hurry up and fire the person. It simply means that you can now determine if there's really any potential for change in the salesperson. As I mentioned before, observable behavior can be totally deceiving. The salesperson who always seems negative and caustic may be dissatisfied with the pay plan or the fact that he or she has to do so much paperwork when he or she wants to be out selling. It's these hidden reasons that make the blueprint model so powerful in assisting sales leaders, like you, in making critical decisions.

What are the benefits of termination? First and foremost, you eliminate paying salespeople who make your life miserable. Taking the decisive steps to get rid of someone who has no potential to change and has very little capacity to perform takes a huge load off your shoulders. That should be enough reason for most people, but there are other benefits as well.

Terminating salespeople does mean you have turnover, which you'd like to avoid, but terminating a salesperson based on a set of specific criteria allows you to keep from making the same mistake again. The value of ridding the team of a morale-killer but gaining the knowledge of how not to hire the same kind of toxic salesperson again far exceeds the unfilled position. The rest of your team will probably be happy to see a bad apple go and won't mind waiting for you to hire a sales champion on the next round. These benchmarks are a crucial step in defining who will be a good fit in your organization.

In the long run, terminating salespeople who are bad fits saves you money. Instead of investing tens of thousands of dollars in training, time, materials, insurance, and salary, you stop the drain that those kinds of salespeople cause to the bottom line. Stringing low performers on with the hope that they will improve not only costs you their direct salary but also lost opportunities, mishandled prospects, and a negative image that can be truly staggering when you calculate the loss. The Blueprint of a Sales Champion model gives you a template for success that can be repeated each time you are in a position where a decision has to be made-for hire, development, or termination.

I could give you all kinds of examples in which a salesperson was a bad fit for the role, but I'd rather make sure you understand the fact that the blueprint model is designed to help you make good decisions regarding your sales team. You can think back to all the people you've ever let go for performance issues, but do you know *why* they were fired beyond the claim that they weren't performing? Without this knowledge from the blueprint, you probably can't in many cases.

As you consider those salespeople, do you find yourself wondering if in fact you made the right decision? This process is hard to swallow sometimes. For it to be effective, you have to know yourself as a leader and your team in a pretty deep way. When the salesperson does have the capacity to perform based on the Blueprint of a Sales Champion model, you have to be ready to look at yourself, the sales leader, as a possibility for the cause of the problem. Remember the case of the salesperson thirty days from termination? The root cause of the performance issue was the sales manager, and it took his willingness to learn more about his sales management role to make his nearly terminated salesperson become the top producer.

Without being able to assess and evaluate yourself as a leader, you'll be missing out on one of the most common problems within sales organizations. You are a lot like a coach. The coach doesn't just show up on Sundays for the game. He's there every day of the week to coach the team and make the decisions. If he simply decided that the quarterback should be benched because he threw four incomplete passes, he'd fail to recognize that he himself was not providing the quarterback with enough coaching. Hands-off sales management rarely yields long-term top-performing salespeople. Before you decide that a member of your sales team is not worth keeping, consider all the factors that come into play, and then you won't have such bad dreams when it comes time to make a decision.

CHAPTER 15

KEEPING THE BEST:
RETAINING SALES CHAMPIONS

It's certainly not your intention to funnel most of your attention every day on problems with salespeople. As a sales leader, it is your job to lead, yet there are literally thousands of people in your role who are resident fire fighters, ready to extinguish any and all problems that come up. Low-performing salespeople tend to start and fuel lots of unnecessary fires. Some days it's fixing client relations; other days it's reviewing and re-explaining standard procedures. If you're spending more time with the salespeople who deliver the fewest results, you're in for a lot more headaches down the road.

This is a difficult balancing act, I know. The squeaky wheel gets the grease almost every time. The salespeople who don't meet their quotas have to be counseled. The Discounter has to be reminded of margins. You need to go on a sales call with the Drill Sergeant to find out the reason why prospects are complaining. As I've said before, being a sales leader is a hard job.

The problem that so many sales leaders run into is that by putting out fires all the time, they actually run the risk of losing those salespeople who are exceptional. Ensuring that you're hiring and training the right people makes a lot of difference, but before you have a team of sales champions you've carefully picked using the blueprint model, it is imperative not to lose the top salespeople currently working for you.

By now, you know what you should be looking for–salespeople who have a Doer/Talker behavior style, who are clear thinkers, whose top values are Economic and Political, and who understand the complex sales process. Keep in mind that again, this is for prospecting-oriented, lead-generating, and new-business-developing outside salespeople. Knowing this can help you make many decisions, from whom to hire to whom to train to whether or not termination is the best choice. But what about those current top salespeople?

Most organizations have top salespeople. Someone has to be the top producer, but do you really know how to maximize his or her potential? Without the Blueprint of a Sales Champion model, your top salespeople, despite the awards and numbers, may not be most efficient. What if you had more information about how and why they were motivated to make more sales? What if you discovered the secret to helping your top performers increase their productivity by 5%? What would that mean to your company? What would that mean to you?

But when do you have the time? The salespeople who make their quotas and consistently bring in new business get the short end of the stick in many sales teams. If everyone who isn't performing as well as the top few superstars gets the bulk of your time, what message does that send to the very people generating the lion's share of the business? The message is perfectly clear to them. As long as they perform, they'll get little attention from the sales leader.

This backward approach to leadership weaves its way into sales organizations everywhere. While you're busy with the Approval-Seekers, Mavericks, and Pinballs, your top salespeople are quietly realizing that there are other organizations out there to work for. It isn't enough to hand out awards and prizes. Sales champions typically want more than that. They want their sales leaders to invest in them, provide what they need, and the rewards that go with being a top producer.

How do you avoid the immediate need to deal with salespeople who aren't performing? The quickest way to determine that is to find out if they really are salvageable. As I mentioned previously, assessing the entire team gives you a unique perspective on the root causes of the failure to meet and exceed goals.

Once you know if your time is being spent wisely, you can take action to eliminate unproductive management hours with salespeople who don't have the capacity to perform. The time you do spend with your "keepers" becomes much more focused and result-oriented, but the question remains about how to increase your odds that your top salespeople will stay with you.

Just as the Blueprint of a Sales Champion model provides targeted information about lower performers, it gives you a complete road map for coaching and retaining sales champions. Superstars need your attention. Just because they lead the team in revenue generation doesn't mean they have everything they need to sell. Tiger Woods is considered by many to be the best golfer in the world, yet despite his status, he invests in his swing coach to help him develop an even stronger game.

Sales champions are really no different than star athletes. They need a coach just as much or more than the salesperson at the bottom of the pack. Plus they need that coach to help them build and strengthen their abilities. Without a strong coach, they can lose their edge, become complacent, or worse, leave for another organization that does offer that kind of attention. We're not talking about micromanagement here. This is about support, leadership, and vision.

You can't afford to lose the best salespeople. Period. Developing them and retaining them should be your top priority. There are many ways to do this, but it all starts with the blueprint. Knowing your sales champions means having the ability to provide them the tools they need to succeed on an individual basis.

Sales champions are typically motivated to act from a values standpoint by making money and exercising influence. Motivation isn't just a function of values though. The term *motivation* tends to be generalized and used as a catch-all.

Regardless, sales leaders want motivated salespeople. You want them to be internally motivated, but motivation is a two-way street. Let me make this point clear. You really can't motivate another person. However, you can create a motivating or demotivating environment for them. Knowing what motivates a salesperson is the key to creating an environment for him or her to perform at a high level. This doesn't mean that as the sales leader, you should give top salespeople whatever they ask for. As with anything, it must be within reason, but when you know that a salesperson is motivated by autonomy and you can provide that, it only makes sense to do so.

The Blueprint of a Sales Champion model provides these answers from a behavioral, cognitive, and values perspective. Behaviorally, sales champions are motivated by actions that allow them to fulfill their needs to be assertive, relational, and energetic. When you know how to create a motivating environment for a salesperson, you unlock potential you might not have known was there. I'm not talking about major overhauls, either. Simple changes can have tremendous effect.

Consider this example. The Blueprint of a Sales Champion model described Ron as a Talker/Doer behavior style. Ron preferred developing strong relationships with prospects and had a very engaging conversational style. His sales manager always spoke to Ron in short, clipped statements, usually on his way down the hall. Ron continued to meet his quotas, but he never offered much information about ongoing issues.

The sales manager, armed with the Blueprint of a Sales Champion model, realized that Ron was motivated by a friendly, relaxing conversation. The sales manager decided to make a change and modify his own behavior when talking with Ron. Now, whenever he needs to talk to Ron, he goes to his office and sits down for a minute of small talk before discussing the issues. The relationship between Ron and his sales manager strengthened because the manager recognized that Ron was motivated by this kind of interactive style. After a short while, Ron began to tell his sales manager more details about things that were happening in the field, which gave the manager a better perspective of his performance. Their relationship improved as well. Simple, yet effective.

Every salesperson, from the top down, has a list of motivating factors related to their particular behavior style. Discovering that your sales champion needs and wants more independence and freedom allows you to adjust your tendency to hold the reins tightly. For another salesperson, you may have to address issues of quality consciousness or recognition for a job well done.

There are also cognitive sources of motivation. Does your

salesperson strongly value personal improvement? If so, provide him with resources to develop himself. Send him to a seminar or buy him books on specific areas of sales development he might like. Is your salesperson motivated by knowing that her role has a function beyond providing her with a paycheck? If this is true, make sure she has opportunities to take part in knowing and implementing the mission of the company.

Being aware of how sales champions see themselves, see the world, and see themselves in the world can offer clues for you to use. When you know these cognitive sources of motivation, you gain insight in an area that is completely outside the realm of observable behavior. It's like having X-ray vision and looking through the outer surface to what's on the inside.

It is the responsibility of the sales leader to know and understand the team. By placing your emphasis and energy into your best people, you set up a new model for managing everyone. Retaining sales champions starts with understanding and then creating a dialogue between you and them. It means satisfying their drivers within the context of the blueprint model. And it means being willing to follow a course of action that may be very different than what you are familiar with.

Retaining sales champions cannot be done from behind a desk. Sales leaders must be able to be right in the trenches with their best people. Working closely on the various motivating factors for your sales champions creates a highly productive and profitable organization. Not having this information can lead to sales champions looking elsewhere.

The discovery that the Blueprint of a Sales Champion model affords you in creating an area for discussion can prove to be very eye-opening. These discussions can lead to ideas and suggestions from your top producers that you may have never considered.

One client of mine was a sales champion. His profile was a perfect match for the role. He had boundless energy, was motivated by money and influence, and was a very clear thinker who had a strong handle on the sales process. In talking to the sales manager, I found out that this salesperson's paperwork was not always accurate or timely.

Once the sales manager and the sales champion begin discussing the results of the Blueprint of a Sales Champion model, the salesperson suggested getting some administrative assistance with his paperwork. The sales manager had never provided any of his salespeople with administrative support like this, but the salesperson convinced him that by not having to spend hours handling back-end paperwork, he could actually sell more. The salesperson's track record showed a strong ability to close sales, so despite never having done anything like it before, the sales manager granted this benefit of administrative support. The result was a greater appreciation between the two and the sales champion did exactly what he said would happen-he made more sales.

The moral of the story is this: By having discussions with your top salespeople about what they want and need to do their jobs better, you uncover opportunities you may not have known were there. The individuals know best what drives them to act, even if they don't always know how to explain it. Using the Blueprint of a Sales Champion model as a springboard gives you and your sales team those definable methods for a highly productive environment.

When those sources of motivation are fulfilled, sales champions and sales leaders feel good about what's happening. The sales champion who wants to make as much money as possible should be given every possible chance to do so within the context of the company goals and structure. When he or she is allowed to do this, he or she will be much more successful, which not only benefits him- or herself but also the company.

WHERE DO I GO FROM HERE?

Now that you've learned about the Blueprint of a Sales Champion model, you're probably asking yourself – "How can I measure my salespeople and sales candidates against the Blueprint model?" The Blueprint of a Sales Champion is based on the Resolution Sales Battery™ (RSB) – an assessment tool that has been tested on salespeople worldwide in a wide variety of industries where prospecting for new business is a key component of the job requirements.

Now you can utilize this proprietary assessment tool and receive a complete and thorough interpretation of the results to help you recruit, refine, and retain Sales Champions for your sales team! Whether you are adding salespeople to your staff and want to avoid the mistakes you've made in the past or you want to develop existing salespeople for greater performance, Resolution Systems, Inc. can help you implement a completely new methodology for your sales organization.

Get the Answer Today

You can discover if your sales candidate or existing salesperson is a Sales Champion by using the Resolution Sales Battery™ assessment. It is completely web-based, so you can assess salespeople anywhere anytime. The results arrive instantly in your e-mail account. There's no waiting!

Once the assessment is completed by your salesperson or sales candidate, *Resolution Systems, Inc.* provides a complete and thorough interpretation. The interpretation assists you in making the best hiring or developmental decision on each salesperson.

<u>There are three ways to get started:</u>
Phone: 1-866-880-5175 (toll-free)
E-mail: info@resolutionsystemsinc.com
Web: www.BlueprintOfASalesChampion.com/contact

Once your online account is set up, we can immediately get you started using our systems for hiring new salespeople, assessing poor performers, identifying developmental areas, determining the best role for an existing salesperson, and bolster your sales training and personal development programs.

All of our consultants are certified to analyze salespeople. Each consultant is a Certified Professional Behavioral Analyst (CPBA) and a Certified Professional Values Analyst (CPVA). With years of experience assisting companies hire and develop top salespeople, they can help you answer the difficult questions.

In addition to the Resolution Sales Battery™ (RSB), we can also assist you in hiring and developing employees in other departments within the organization. Our other assessment tools include:

- Resolution Sales Management Battery™ (RSMB)

- Resolution Customer Service Battery™ (RCSB)

- Resolution Management Battery™ (RMB)

- Resolution General Employment Battery™ (RGEB)

- Resolution Team Building Battery™ (RTBB)

In conjunction with the assessments, Resolution Systems, Inc. consults with sales teams and advises salespeople and sales managers on how to increase performance by focusing more attention on the internal components of individuals. Because most sales assessments measure external elements like personality or behavior style only, they are an incomplete portrayal of future performance capability. Basing your hiring and development strategies on the Blueprint model, you can end the cycle of a purely random process.

Hire Barrett Riddleberger

Barrett Riddleberger, CEO, is a professional business speaker and is available for keynote speaking engagements for national and regional sales meetings. To get more information about hiring Barrett Riddleberger to speak to your organization, please visit www.riddleberger.com.

If you're looking for solutions for recruiting, sales training, or sales management training, you can find out more information at www.resolutionsystemsinc.com. You can also sign up for The Resolution Report, a monthly e-newsletter specifically designed for sales leadership.

Resolution Systems, Inc. combines the power of the Blueprint of a Sales Champion model with straightforward, "No Fluff" training and development to provide organizations with the most consistent and accurate sales strategies, allowing them to compete in the marketplace with greater success.

If you have additional questions regarding our assessments or any of our services, please call us toll-free at 866-880-5175 or e-mail at info@resolutionsystemsinc.com.

A FINAL THOUGHT

There are many things you have to consider as a sales leader. Your job is multifaceted, and often it's tough to juggle all the balls at once. Regardless of your current situation within the organization, the demanding task of making accurate and profitable decisions about salespeople doesn't have to be steeped in frustration and exorbitant costs. Top performers, the ones with the capacity to perform in the outside sales role, can be discovered.

Whether you are in a hiring phase because of company growth or you're holding steady and want to bolster your existing team or if the economy has required you to cut back and keeping only the best is imperative, you have a reliable, repeatable system for ensuring that your decisions will be based on measurable data, not intuition and hopes.

The Blueprint of a Sales Champion model allows you to make decisions about salespeople in a way that's fundamentally sound. Behavior style, cognitive structure, values structure, and selling skills are the four determining factors that contribute to (or deter from) a salesperson's ability to function as an outside sales role. Having this information prior to hiring "the perfect candidate" can make the difference between a marginal player and a sales champion. Likewise, measuring an existing salesperson against the blueprint can reveal numerous reasons for problematic issues and what to do about them.

The relief my clients have felt in knowing that they can count on the results of this model is a tremendous load off their shoulders. Sales leaders around the country say the same things. They want strong salespeople to help their companies compete in the marketplace. They want to end the cycle of continual turnover. They want to provide their teams with strong leadership that gets results. Harnessing the power of the Blueprint of a Sales Champion model can do that for every single salesperson you hire and retain.

It's not magic, although it may seem magical when your next hire actually does perform at a high level or your mediocre salesperson, whom you were ready to fire, turns into your #1 producer. It doesn't have to be that dramatic either. Changing a few minor tactics or management strategies can turn an otherwise marginal salesperson into someone you genuinely appreciate having on your team.

It doesn't always happen overnight though. The problems typically don't arrive at the front door at 8 am on a Monday morning. Making the transition from a purely behavior- and skills-based mentality to the more comprehensive "blueprint" model takes both time and willingness to redirect old habits. You don't have to give up your use of perception and intuition, but you do have to be willing to examine yourself as well as your team within the context of the overall corporate mission and goals.

Because the Blueprint of a Sales Champion model is designed for the sales leader in relation to the salesperson, measuring your salespeople against it will provide you with clues and directives for the individual. The role of your particular salespeople stays relatively the same, and knowing what characteristics are specifically key to your organization gives you even greater control over filling those positions with people who are most likely to succeed in that environment.

The success of the Blueprint of a Sales Champion model does require the commitment of a relationship—one between you and each one of your salespeople. It is a device to assist you in making those decisions with a hands-on approach to leadership. Where there is an open dialogue and constructive communication, there will be a greater chance for a highly productive sales environment.

Even though the measurements and formulas for providing this invaluable data are highly complex, the concept is simple. Hiring, developing, and retaining top salespeople–sales champions –every time using the blueprint is the secret to maximizing productivity and reducing your own headaches with never-ending problems.

A builder never begins a house without an accurate and detailed plan for construction. That blueprint provides everything a builder needs to make that house a successful venture–on the outside and on the inside.

If you're tired of hiring and employing salespeople who only look good on the exterior but fail to measure up to your standards for excellence, you need to start building your team with a complete plan–the Blueprint of a Sales Champion.

THE BLUEPRINT OF A SALES CHAMPION

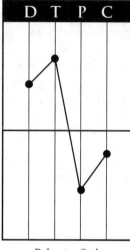

Behavior Style

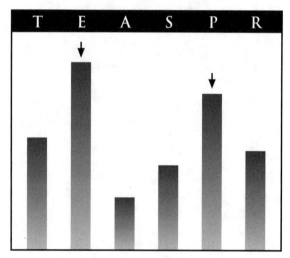

Value Structure

The Blueprint Of A Sales Champion

Cognitive Structure

Strong Clarity and Focus
- Self-Starting Capacity
- Handling Rejection
- Personal Accountability
- Emotional Control
- Persistence
- Self-Confidence
- Handling Stress
- Goal Direction
- Results Orientation
- *+ over 70 more attributes*

Selling Skills

Score 40+ on Selling Skills
- Prospecting
- Building Value
- Asking Questions
- Qualifying Buyers
- Developing Trust
- Closing
- Presentation Skills
- Validation
- Pre-Call Planning
- Minimizing Risk

I would like to acknowledge the contributions of *Target Training International*, *Performance Benchmarking* and *The Brooks Group* for the research contained in this book. All of the research is used by permission.

The Personal Interests and Values™ profile is used by permission Copyright © 1990 - 2001 *Target Training International.*

The Managing For Success™ Behavior profile is used by permission. Copyright © 1984 - 2001 *Target Training International.*

References to the Attributes Index™ report is used by permission. Copyright © 1989 – 2003 *The Brooks Group.*
© 2003 Innermetrix

The terms Doer, Talker, Pacer and Controller are used by permission by William T. Brooks.

ABOUT THE AUTHOR

Barrett Riddleberger has spent years analyzing what makes salespeople perform at the highest levels. As a sales analyst, speaker, and author, Barrett has helped companies throughout North America to recruit, refine, and retain Sales Champions.

Originally from Charleston, SC, Barrett Riddleberger is the CEO of Resolution Systems, Inc., a sales recruiting, training, and consulting firm, located in Greensboro, NC. Barrett received a BA in Communications from the University of North Carolina at Greensboro and also holds the designations of Certified Professional Behavior Analyst and Certified Professional Values Analyst. Additionally, he is a Charter Facilitator for the *Og Mandino Success System* (*The Greatest Salesman in the World Sales Program.*)

He has delivered his custom keynote programs all over North America and his direct, engaging style has given sales leadership a new, effective method for answering the question, "How do I build a great sales team after I've tried everything else?"

Barrett is the author of Blueprint of a Sales Champion in which he details the dynamics of how top-performing salespeople are constructed and how sales management can utilize the power of the Sales Champion model in all areas of hiring, developing, and retaining the very best salespeople.

In addition to a busy schedule of speaking to and consulting with sales organizations, Barrett also sits on the Board of Directors of *Faith In Focus, Inc.* – an apologetics ministry providing a reasoned defense for the true gospel of Jesus Christ.

Barrett is married and has three children. Before becoming CEO of Resolution Systems, Inc, he developed a proprietary sales-force automation software system called Spitfire. He is a former air personality for a classic rock station and a former free-lance television photojournalist.

As a high school football player, he played for famed coach John McKissick, who recorded the most wins (over 500) in the history of the game. There he learned the life principles of what it takes to create a winning team.

Barrett's goal is to educate sales organizations about the supreme importance of the human performance element when it comes to salespeople. Whether he's speaking to a room full of executives, motivating a sales force or delivering one of his monthly tele-seminars, his message is clear: there is a formula for recruiting, refining and retaining Sales Champions.